# How to Succeed in College!

## Choosing a Major, Transferring, and Completing Your Degree in Four Years or Less

Mark J. Mach

*Published in partnership with the*
*National Society of Collegiate Scholars*

ScarecrowEducation
Lanham, Maryland • Toronto • Oxford
2004

Published in partnership with the
National Society of Collegiate Scholars

Published in the United States of America
by ScarecrowEducation
An imprint of The Rowman & Littlefield Publishing Group, Inc.
4501 Forbes Boulevard, Suite 200, Lanham, Maryland 20706
www.scarecroweducation.com

PO Box 317
Oxford
OX2 9RU, UK

British Library Cataloguing in Publication Information Available

**Library of Congress Cataloging-in-Publication Data**

Mach, Mark J., 1972–
  How to succeed in college! : choosing a major, transferring, and completing
your degree in four years or less / Mark J. Mach.
      p. cm.
  "Published in partnership with the National Society of Collegiate Scholars."
  Includes bibliographical references.
  ISBN 1-57886-162-4 (pbk. : alk. paper)
  1. College student orientation—United States.  I. National Society of
Collegiate Scholars. II. Title.
LB2343.32.M27 2004
378.1'98—dc22

                                                        2004010464

⊗™ The paper used in this publication meets the minimum requirements of
American National Standard for Information Sciences—Permanence of Paper
for Printed Library Materials, ANSI/NISO Z39.48-1992.
Manufactured in the United States of America.

# Contents

# Preface

College can be an exciting and stressful time of life. These years are filled with potential promises of intellectual, social, and personal fulfillment, oftentimes unparalleled during other phases of our lives. Indeed, one would be extremely hard-pressed to find another period of life that offers such opportunities for growth as does the college experience. Professionals who study college students sometimes even claim the college years as being the best times in a person's life.

Unfortunately, this glowing portrait of the college ideal does not always match the harsh reality of life in today's colleges and universities. College can also be a time of unsurpassed struggles, pain, and disillusionment. However, despite this stark reality, the proverbial silver lining does exist and can be accessible to you. Among a host of other important characteristics, planning, organization, dedication, commitment, motivation, and perseverance are major keys that will contribute to your success in college.

The ideas in this book serve as guidelines in assisting you during the planning and organizational phases of your college career. Although this book will not be able to help you in the dedication, commitment, motivation, and perseverance that are also essential qualities for ensuring your success in college, it should nevertheless serve as an important guide in helping you clarify your own goals and aspirations in college.

Primary audiences for this book include:

- High school students.
- College students deciding on a major or considering transferring to another college.
- College students already in a college and major of their choice but want affirmation of these choices.
- College students looking for ways to achieve continuing success in college.

Other audiences who might find this book useful include parents and other supporters of high school and college students. This book is also intended for both traditional and nontraditional-age college students.

I wish you the very best as you embark or continue on your journey toward a successful experience in college.

# 1

## The College Ideal

Colleges and universities publicize themselves remarkably well. They provide students with an abundance of brochures, pamphlets, and letters starting in the fall of one's junior year in high school. By the fall semester of my senior year in high school, my bedroom floor was literally piled with stacks of these college brochures, pamphlets, and letters. Eventually, I sorted through these huge piles, sent out my applications, and anxiously awaited the eventual responses, and hopefully, acceptance letters. By January of my senior year in high school, I had been offered admission to a campus of the giant California State University system. I promptly accepted their offer of admission, attended freshman orientation that summer, and began my college career on September 4, 1990.

Once I was "in" and had made my final decision to attend this college, I soon became aware that my problems had just begun! Almost immediately, I regretted my rash decision to attend this particular college. With hindsight, I wish I had more thoroughly and thoughtfully examined the characteristics of my college before mailing in my acceptance letter. Unfortunately, at the time, I had no idea what to expect out of any college, let alone the one I would soon be attending. This situation caused me much unnecessary tension, anxiety, and stress—and it was a burden I should not have carried in the first place. I want to help you avoid the same painful mistake I made many years ago.

I first knew that something was definitely wrong when I attended the open house of my new university, held in the spring preceding my entrance as a freshman. Things certainly seemed promising at first. It was an unusually warm and sunny spring morning when my father and I set out for the campus. I had taken that Friday off from school so I could attend this important event. I truly felt this was going to be a great day. The drive to the campus usually took about three hours, so there was plenty of time for me to ponder the upcoming events of that day. By the time we arrived at the campus, it was almost noon, and yet the day for me had hardly begun.

Have you ever sensed an immediate feeling of dread and disappointment from the moment you set foot in a certain place? Well, this was exactly how I felt as soon as we drove into a parking lot on campus. I felt something was just not right. I immediately sensed I did not belong there. In a way, my mind was saying, "Mark, you're not supposed to be here! You fool! What are you doing here? Get out of here!" At that point, I chose not to listen to my inner voice.

After we had secured a parking spot underneath a shady tree, my father and I walked over to a service building on the south side of campus. We asked for directions to the day's festivities. We walked over to the student center, where it was soon announced that another campus tour was about to begin. Maybe now, I thought to myself, I would get a better glimpse of the campus. Perhaps now I would begin feeling better about the school. My father and I waited our turn to visit the rest of the campus grounds on a student-led tour.

The tour itself lasted less than an hour. We were first shown the side of campus we were currently on, which consisted of several buildings from various departments, the library, and the performing arts theatre. The final part of the tour, the tour of the dormitories, was the part I was most nervous about seeing. I still get anxious thinking about it even today, many years later!

There was so much I did not see of the campus that might have saved me from future agony, had I only been allowed to see it! We saw only a few department buildings and were led inside only one dormitory wing—but the school itself consisted of many departments and six dormitory buildings. The dorm rooms that we did end up seeing were suites on a designated "quiet floor," which really were not representative of a true picture of the realities of life on campus. I had a bad feeling about what I had gotten myself into. I had just accepted an admission offer to a university I did not like.

That afternoon many years ago, after I had looked around on campus, I felt completely disgusted with myself. I had chosen to attend a university that seemed at great odds with my personality and college goals. To this day, I still feel cheated over what I did and did not get to see while on the campus tour. Unfortunately, I had not been very flexible in deciding which college to attend. One of the greatest assets you have in selecting a college, either as a prospective freshman or college transfer student, is your flexibility.

## STEPS TO SUCCESS

1. Be flexible when choosing a college to attend.
2. Apply to a minimum of six to eight schools.
3. Make a list of ideal vs. realistic college qualities.
4. Do not rely solely on tours for information; ask questions.
5. Rank your colleges and use your intuition.

## STEP 1: BE FLEXIBLE WHEN CHOOSING A COLLEGE TO ATTEND

Perhaps you might not believe it, but as a high school student or as a prospective college transfer student you have tremendous flexibility in choosing a college that will best meet your needs.

The biggest problem in making a blind decision over where to attend college is that it is sometimes difficult to transfer to another school once you are already attending a college or university. If you are already going to another school, on average you are facing at least two more years of waiting before you will be able to transfer. One option—choosing to attend a two-year junior or community college—is certainly possible if you absolutely cannot stand your present college or university. (I address this option more fully in a later chapter.) If this is not a realistic choice for you, then you can pretty much bank on the two-year waiting period.

Always remember that there is no law against applying to many different schools. Generally speaking, with the exception of overeager parents or idealistic friends, nobody will care where you apply to or how many applications you send out. At the same time, this does not mean you should just dive in and randomly apply to many schools. There is an organizational and planning strategy that can help you apply smartly, not blindly. The scenario I faced in college many years ago will help me to further illustrate this picture for you. I want you to make a carefully planned and intelligent decision of where you go to college, rather than a random choice. While a certain amount of luck is sometimes needed in getting into a school you like, getting into the college of your choice amounts to much more than just plain luck.

When I graduated from high school, I left myself with only two choices of where I might be able to go to college. During my senior year in high school, I was very determined to move out of my parents' home. Because of my stubbornness, I did not allow anyone to convince me of the wisdom of attending a two-year junior or community college. Theoretically, I knew I could still choose to apply to a two-year junior or community college, even up through the first few weeks of my freshman year in college. I believed I could easily transfer schools later but I was determined to weather the possible storm at my new college. I believed I had little choice otherwise. I really wanted to experience life away from home, so the two-year school option was immediately tossed out, leaving me with the choice of sticking it out at my new college.

I naïvely thought that randomly applying to three schools—the California State University campus and two campuses of the University of California—was plenty. I was totally surprised when I received rejection letters from both University of California campuses. Intelligently applying to six to eight colleges is your best bet of having at least three to four good choices open to you, but you must really use your brain in making your first-round selections. You will greatly appreciate this flexibility in choosing a compatible school when the time comes for you to make your final decision. If you apply only to a couple of schools, your choices will be narrowed considerably, and your flexibility to choose an ideal college or university will be restricted and compromised. You will sell yourself short if you are not flexible.

## STEP 2: APPLY TO A MINIMUM OF SIX TO EIGHT SCHOOLS

Remember, though, this does not mean you should randomly or blindly apply to six to eight schools. This can be just as bad as applying to only a few colleges in an intelligent manner. It could be even worse, considering the fact that college applications take a lot of time and hard work, not to mention the money involved in application fees. If you can afford it, try applying to as many schools as possible. Obviously, the more places you apply to, the more choices you will probably have available. Statisticians often term this concept the "law of averages." The law of averages simply means chance alone will make it likely that you will receive more acceptance letters by applying to many schools. However, also remember there is an intelligent, organized, and strategic method you should use when applying.

Let us assume you will be applying to six to eight colleges or universities. Of these schools, you should apply to two "dream" schools, two to four "realistic but good" schools, and two very realistic or "safe" schools. By intelligently applying in this manner, you might have a golden opportunity to not only attend a "dream" school but you will also have several ideal "backup" schools, just in case you are not accepted by your top-choice schools. There are never too many colleges at which you can apply, but there are definitely too few. If you are thinking of applying to fewer than three schools, I strongly recommend that you involve your family, teachers, and guidance counselors and explore ways you can expand that list.

Making lists for tasks you need to complete can be tremendously useful. If you have ever had a lot of homework and also have a lot of other events going on in your life, how easy is it to remember what chapter you are supposed to read for history? Or what problems you are supposed to do for math? Or when something else is due? Making lists is extremely useful when it comes to choosing an ideal college. After you have your acceptance letters in hand, and even while you are still applying to schools, you should be able to list your ideal characteristics of college on paper. Compare your ideal list to the actual colleges you are considering. Does your ideal list match your realistic list of colleges and their qualities? It definitely should. Otherwise, you will seriously want to rethink your decision to accept the offer of admission.

## STEP 3: MAKE A LIST OF IDEAL VS. REALISTIC COLLEGE QUALITIES

I had never made these lists until I decided to transfer colleges — but how I now wish I had written some things down first! When I was first considering transferring, a topic we will cover in more depth in chapters 4 and

5, I made out a standard list of my ideal college qualities. I included several dimensions on this list, as shown in appendix A, but you should definitely consider including more characteristics if this suits your own personal, academic, and professional ideals. Appendix A also shows you how to create an objective method to score and rank the qualities of your prospective colleges.

Most of your prospective colleges will have statistics on the criteria shown in appendix A. Be sure and check your local college, public library, or the Internet for more information on how to interpret these statistics. I strongly recommend that you take at least three tours of each college campus you are seriously considering. Sometimes, these tours can help you to verify these otherwise impersonal and questionable statistics. This is especially true if you are willing to carefully scrutinize what you see while on the tour. Does your tour seem limited in any way? Or does it seem like your tour is giving you a good glimpse of the campus? See if you can go at different times of the day. Night and weekend tours of campus can be especially revealing. Try and keep the scheduled, and oftentimes scripted, staff- or student-led tours down to an absolute minimum. While these formal tours can occasionally be informative, they are more often incomplete at best and misleading at worst. You will not get a true view of your prospective college if you rely only on a formal tour, given at restricted times of the day, for most of your information about a college or university.

## STEP 4: DO NOT RELY SOLELY ON TOURS FOR INFORMATION

I know it sounds a bit intimidating at first, but it is almost always a good idea to tour the prospective colleges either alone or with a trusted friend or relative, at least once. If you choose to go with someone else, make sure that person has your best interests in mind and is as objective as possible. Asking students who are walking around on campus about the quality of the school can be tremendously informative. Students who are not held accountable by campus payroll and who do not have to follow a scripted tour, followed by scripted answers, can provide you with insight you would have never gotten on a formal campus tour. Student-led campus tours, as I illustrated earlier, simply will not usually give you the most accurate picture of the college or the answers you may be seeking. The bottom line is this: tour guides are there to make the school look good. This is generally why most schools hire students to work as tour guides only if they feel they can completely trust them to say only positive things about the school. However, students walking around randomly on campus will give you much better insight into the reality of campus life.

With this latter method of picking out random students, you will find students who will boast about the superiority of the college, disgruntled students who want to overthrow the administration of the school, and students falling everywhere else. Your new college will be your home away from home for a while, so you can and should know something about the school you may be attending. Ask about any aspects of the campus that may be bothering you at the moment. The students I have questioned on a number of different campuses have always been helpful and friendly. It is far better and wiser to suffer from fleeting embarrassment by questions you may be afraid of asking, rather than to suffer through long years of disillusionment and regret over a poor choice of college. Try to pick out the early weeks of the semester (or quarter) to visit the campuses, when it is much more likely to find students with time to sit down and answer all your questions. Appendix B shows some sample questions you might want to ask students at your prospective campuses.

## STEP 5: RANK YOUR COLLEGES AND USE YOUR INTUITION

Now, it is time to finish collecting your data on your college selections. Following the directions in appendix A, try using the rating scale shown, in order to see how well your prospective colleges measure up to your ideal college standards. Be as honest as possible in your judgment. It will hurt you immensely if you fudge even just a little bit on your ratings. Use the rating scale found in appendix A on each of your college qualities that you have listed. Ten, for example, would exactly match your ideal college criteria, five would be halfway toward matching your ideal standards, and one would be a quality that is completely opposite from matching your ideal college standards. Use your best judgment to decide how much weight to apply to each of these characteristics. Add up the scores, divide by the total number of your listed college qualities, and your answer will give you that college's individual rating. Then, compare scores. The highest average score should be your first college admissions offer to accept. If there is a tie in your ratings, or if you do not like the way your score for the first-choice college turned out, either recalculate your ratings accordingly, or use your intuition to decide on the winner.

Either way, rating the schools is a fair and objective way to choose a college. However, your intuition or good feeling alone about a particular school should definitely take precedence over the purely objective ratings. My fault in choosing my first college was that I did not adhere to either method. I was neither passionate nor objective about accepting my admissions letter. I strongly urge you to use both an objective rating scale and your intuition in choosing your first choice of college.

Once you are in and have finally accepted an offer that you truly want, I sincerely congratulate you. Choosing to attend a particular college or university, either as a freshman or as a transfer student, is a difficult and arduous task. I now invite you to take a glimpse into the reality of life at your college and a choice that is perhaps even more challenging: choosing a compatible major.

# 2

# Choosing a Compatible Major: The Fundamentals

**Y**our initial choice of a major—although the very name itself implies a major decision of sorts—usually will not make or break your entire college career or your life. A major is, after all, just one of the many substantial parts that make up the entire spectrum of the college experience. It should serve as a great comfort for you to know that many college graduates end up in fields completely unrelated to their college major—and they still enjoy their career after college. Many graduate students have even chosen to enter fields entirely different from what they chose as a major during their undergraduate years. Indeed, one is hard-pressed to find a group of students who stuck with a field of study on into graduate school, professional school, or their eventual career.

Especially for liberal arts students, but even increasingly so in the sciences, majors are designed to give undergraduates a broad survey, not an intensive study, of the chosen major. Most colleges and universities today have what are known as general education, or core, requirements. These requirements make college students spend much of their first two years taking courses outside their intended major—assuming that a student has even declared a major at this early stage.

Two years is a substantial amount of time to decide what area of school interests you. At the risk of alienating some parents and career-minded friends, I will go out on a limb and say that it is perfectly okay to remain undecided on a major—at least for the first year of college, and usually for the first two years. Decisions made under tremendous pressure are generally not the ones we look back on as the best ones we have ever made. Have you ever bought a big, expensive item, such as a computer or a car, and immediately afterwards regretted your quick purchase? This feeling of "buyer's remorse" can definitely apply to your choice of a college major—and your active decision to remain undecided during your first year or two of college. Deciding on a major does not at all mean you will be forever bound to a particular field. For the vast majority of us, what we chose to major in is not even directly related to what we are currently doing in our professional careers.

## STEPS TO SUCCESS

1. Take a wide variety of classes your freshman year.
2. Do not take any upper-division courses just yet.
3. Never choose a major based solely on difficulty.
4. Know the policy regarding declaring a major.
5. If transferring, declare a major soon.
6. Complete your major requirements within three years.

## STEP 1: TAKE A WIDE VARIETY OF CLASSES YOUR FRESHMAN YEAR

In general, expect to spend at least the first year of college exploring possible choices for a major. One of the best ways in which you can successfully accomplish this goal is to take a wide variety of general education courses during your first two years in college. In a later chapter on transferring, you will learn how to explore the best ways to fulfill major requirements.

During the first semester of my freshman year in college, I believed I would be best suited for a major in economics. After all, I thought to myself, I enjoyed my economics class as a senior in high school. At the time, my mind seemed to equate high school-level classes with college-level classes. Well, I soon learned what many college freshmen eventually learn—college is a whole new ball game. After enrolling in an introductory economics class during my first semester, I found the subject was not at all to my personal liking. I did not enjoy the class or the subject matter. Economics was not something I could see myself studying during my four years in college. The first sign I needed to change my major came after I purchased the textbook for the course. I understood the material as I read through the first few chapters, but I just could not "get into" the reading.

My lack of enthusiasm with my economics class soon translated into an unhappy economics major. I did not want to study for my upcoming tests in that class, since the material was so lackluster to me. The one course in my intended major was, in essence, being shoved aside for other courses. I soon found my introductory psychology class much more suitable for my personal tastes. Soon after this discovery, I started devoting more time reading about behaviorism than I did about supply, demand, and inflation. Even though I procrastinated, I did study for my economics tests, and I did end up receiving a fairly respectable B− in the course. However, studying for this class was a nightmare for me. Luckily, I happened to be taking a wide variety of general education classes that semester, so I was not limiting myself only to economics. My first semester schedule included such diverse subjects as the introductory economics and introductory psychology classes, introductory humanities, American history, and introductory archery.

Appendix C shows sample schedules for freshmen and sophomores. These schedules show progress being made toward completing both general education and major requirements. Please note, however, that these are intended to serve as sample schedules only. General education and major course requirements may vary substantially at each college or university.

Although I was completely turned off by economics, I discovered I was absolutely intrigued by the psychology class I happened to be taking during my first semester in college. The professor who taught the course was so interesting and charismatic as a person that I could not help but like his class. The possibilities of a major in psychology seemed exciting to me. Solely on the basis of this class, I declared psychology as a minor later that semester. During spring semester of my freshman year, psychology was to become my new major.

## STEP 2: DO NOT TAKE ANY
## UPPER-DIVISION COURSES JUST YET

That same spring semester of my freshman year, I wanted to take an upper-division class in criminal justice. The course I wanted to take sounded very interesting. In addition to learning the course material, I also learned another lesson from this class. Later, I would find out that taking upper-level classes can sometimes be a hindrance if you decide to transfer. As it turned out, the upper-division criminal justice course was the only class I did not get full transfer credit from.

I should add here that your last two years of college will be devoted almost exclusively to upper-division work. Try not to rush into taking these types of courses. It is far better for you to be well prepared to take these types of classes as you mature as a college student. Usually, during your first two years of college, you are not academically ready to take these types of courses. During that spring semester of my freshman year, I happened to take the upper-level course in criminal justice concurrently with a lower-level course in the same field.

## STEP 3: NEVER CHOOSE A MAJOR
## BASED SOLELY ON DIFFICULTY

It turned out that my lower-division course was somewhat interesting, not to mention fairly simplistic—so I decided to declare criminal justice as my new major. Unfortunately, unlike psychology, I discovered I did not feel comfortable in the criminal justice major from the very beginning. My upper-division course in criminal justice that spring semester was pretty boring for me, so I felt as if I had wasted a lot of my time. Declare a major only out of interest for the material or the subject area itself—never declare a major only because the course work is easy. Always challenge yourself, especially in your major.

## STEP 4: KNOW THE POLICY REGARDING DECLARING A MAJOR

Once you have reached a decision on a major, it is then necessary to find out what the policy at your college is on declaring and/or changing a major. At most California State University campuses, and at most two-year junior and community colleges, it is fairly easy to declare or change a major within your first year, and usually through the first full two years, of college. At my California State University campus, I was simply required to fill out a few lines on one page of paper, sign at the bottom, and turn the form in at the Registrar's Office. A few weeks later, a letter came in the mail formally welcoming me to my new major. At most junior and community colleges, the procedure for declaring and/or changing a major is often just as easy. You simply write in the name of your new major, sign at the bottom, and turn the form in.

There is a caveat to this ideal picture of declaring and/or changing majors. Some colleges and universities have what they call "impacted majors." This means there is very limited space available for students wishing to declare these majors. Not every student who wants to declare a major classified as being impacted will be admitted. Departments with impacted majors often require students to have certain minimum grade point averages in order to be admitted to the major. Some departments will even make prospective students take an exam before they can declare an impacted major. Impacted majors are fairly common occurrences at most colleges and universities, so it is always wise to check with the department or division office of the major you are interested in declaring before you submit the actual paperwork.

Some colleges and universities allow you to declare more than one major at a time, so check the policy of your own school if you plan on having double or multiple majors. As another caveat, I want to caution you that it is not always easy to change majors. This is particularly true depending on the department and school you are enrolled in. At the University of California, where I later transferred to and graduated from, it can be more difficult to change an initial choice of major and may therefore require more up-front commitment on your part. This reality holds true for most types of majors on the campuses of the University of California. The paperwork is considerably lengthier, and you are usually required to meet with the department office, the school or division office, and an academic advisor. Simply signing a form and turning it in to the Registrar's Office will not work at some institutions, particularly the more highly selective colleges and universities. Private schools also tend to make it more of a hassle to change majors.

## STEP 5: IF TRANSFERRING, DECLARE A MAJOR SOON

If you are considering transferring, it is especially important for you to make a firm commitment to a major as early as possible in your college career. When I first transferred to a two-year community college, in order to later transfer to a campus of the University of California system, I made it a point to outline all my lower-division general education and major requirements before transferring. I was able to obtain a list of the required general education courses, along with courses in my major, that were necessary for transferring to the University of California. If you are a two-year junior or community college student and you plan on transferring to a four-year school, you should see an academic advisor for a list of transferable lower-division general education and major requirements.

In general, although most colleges, including schools that accept transfer students, will not expect a firm commitment to a major until the beginning of your junior year, it is a sound and wise idea to start committing yourself to a field of study as early as possible after your first year of college. Preferably, you will want to do this during the first quarter or semester of your sophomore year. This way, you will be ready and able to transfer schools upon completion of your lower-division general education and major requirements at the end of your sophomore year.

## STEP 6: COMPLETE YOUR MAJOR REQUIREMENTS WITHIN THREE YEARS

Not only is this plan helpful in knowing which lower-division general education and major requirements you will need to fulfill for transferring, but also, as I will explain in later chapters, this plan allows you to take most of your upper-division course requirements during your junior year. In turn, this leaves your senior year open to do all sorts of interesting things within your major, such as field study, internships, research opportunities, and even possible teaching assistant positions. The last thing you will want to do during your senior year is take more classes to fulfill major requirements. Independent study projects, as I will explain in a future chapter, will be rewarding academically, intellectually, and possibly, career-wise.

# 3

## Choosing a Compatible Major: The Process

Contrary to popular belief, there really is no "right" or "wrong" major. Colleges and universities originally designed the concept of a major, or interest of study, for the sole purpose of matching your interests with the realities of structured academic life in college. Believe it or not, majors were actually designed for your convenience! Yes, choosing a major can create a lot of headaches and there will be times during this process when you will be asking yourself if all this stress is really worth it in the end. Do not worry, a commitment like this does pay off, as I will be explaining and illustrating throughout this chapter. Even if your choice of a major does not guarantee you a dream job after graduation, it will still be worth it.

Imagine for a moment if there were no majors in college. Then, imagine how potential employers would react when they found out your college degree basically consisted of nothing specific and you had no academic field of interest. Get the picture? Their response would most likely

---

### STEPS TO SUCCESS

1. Clarify your academic and professional goals.
2. Write down as many of your interests as you can.
3. Rank your interests in order of their importance.
4. Look at descriptions of majors in college catalogs.
5. Make a decision.

be this rather sarcastic one, "That's terrific! And guess what? Our company also has no specific job for you."

## STEP 1: CLARIFY YOUR ACADEMIC AND PROFESSIONAL GOALS

While there is no single "right" or "wrong" major for you, there is a major out there that is pretty specific in matching your interests, needs, and abilities. In this chapter, we look at ways to figure out how you can match your intellectual, personal, and career goals with a college major. One of the questions I repeatedly emphasize throughout this discussion is the importance of asking yourself where your priorities are in your decision to pursue a college degree. Take a moment to ask yourself the following very important question and the related questions that stem from it. Be brutally honest in your answers to the following:

Do you know why you are in, or are planning to attend, college?

- Is it merely to achieve a strong, active social life?
- Is it out of respect for pleasing your parents?
- Is it for a higher personal purpose?

If you are leaning mostly toward the last question, you are more than ready to begin seriously examining the prospects of choosing a compatible major.

The first issue you must raise with yourself when choosing a major is this: are your academic goals mainly intellectual in scope, career-oriented, personally related issues, or a combination of these areas? In other words, how important is achieving personal growth to you? How important is finding a good job after graduation going to be for you? Where is your focus? What are your priorities? Are you someone who wants it all? Do you have a more realistic picture of where you want to be within a few years after graduating from college?

Always remember this very important but far too often overlooked fact: college students often do not end up in career fields directly related to their major. Most of us end up changing careers at least a few times during our lives. This latter issue is not the result of making mistakes and bad decisions while we were in college. Rather, it is because life is all about growth and change. What interests you as a twenty-year-old will not necessarily still interest you as a forty-year-old. It could, but not always, and certainly not for most of us.

Now, take a moment to picture your graduation day. Is the sun shining brightly? Is there a single cloud in the sky? Is it a warm, but not too hot, day? Is there a gentle breeze blowing? Now, try to find yourself in the crowd of graduates. There you are! Try visualizing what your mind-set will be like on that day. Will you be looking back with thankfulness for the opportunity you have had to explore new intellectual horizons? Do you think you will have adopted a new philosophy of life? Or will you be anxious and ready to make your mark on the world right away? Possibly, you might feel most or all of these things. The more things you feel now, however, I guarantee the more difficult it will be for you to find a perfectly compatible major. This will be your first and most important step in the whole process of choosing a compatible major:

As a very general rule (the exceptions are plenty), the humanities, social sciences, and natural sciences are fundamentally geared more toward your achieving intellectual growth and development. The primary focus of these "liberal arts" fields is not on your gaining a job in a directly related field upon graduation. On the other hand, fields such as business administration, education, engineering, architecture, nursing, pharmacy, journalism, social welfare, and allied health are generally more career-oriented fields. These areas of study are often more payable in the form of a directly related job after graduation. This does not mean you will not be able to find employment if you decide to major in the liberal arts; nor does it imply that you cannot gain intellectual growth and development by majoring in more career-oriented fields. Rather, it calls your attention to majors that have historically tended to be more career-oriented.

In general, career-oriented majors have a curriculum that is more applied and vocational in nature. Liberal arts (especially in the social sciences) lean more toward theoretically based ideas and insight. Liberal arts majors are certainly "employable" and "marketable" majors if we look broadly enough at the reading, writing, and critical thinking skills students gain from these types of majors. However, students with liberal arts majors will generally require additional years of schooling beyond the bachelor's degree in order to successfully enter a directly related field. There are many exceptions, but this is the general rule in many academic fields in the liberal arts.

Many majors require a graduate education in order for you to advance in your respective field. Some majors even require a graduate degree for an entry-level position in the field. For example, if you are an English major, it may be difficult for you to get a position right out of college that is directly related to your major. In psychology, as was the case with me, I went from counseling and teaching while still a graduate student, to teaching once I had completed graduate school, and back to counseling to start off my career. It was very difficult for me as a recent college graduate to find directly related employment in psychology. For liberal arts majors, it will generally take an advanced degree in order for you to obtain professional work that is directly related to your major. However, at the same time, you will also be discovering some organizations that want you nonetheless, because most liberal arts students have excellent communication and critical thinking skills. This expertise includes skills in writing, speaking, and expression in the arts. These are qualities employers will always be looking for in their prospective employees.

So your options are still plentiful if you choose to major in a liberal arts field. However, you will also need to be flexible in terms of the types of careers you are open to learning. If you are a student majoring in certain vocational areas, such as business administration, education, engineering, and so forth, chances are good that you will be able to find directly related employment within your field upon graduation from college. Again, I do not want to imply here that liberal arts students cannot gain directly related employment immediately upon graduation from college; however, it will probably be more difficult, if not highly improbable, for them to do so. Still, this should not necessarily affect your choice of a major. There are many good and well-paying options for college graduates who majored in liberal arts fields. I strongly suggest visiting your campus career center or local public library in order to discover the career opportunities that are relevant for your own major.

Most of you will want to grow intellectually during your college experience. In addition, you also want to have bright prospects for gaining satisfying future employment. These are perfectly fine and very worthy goals. However, because of these lofty ideals, your planning will be considerably more difficult and require more dedication and organization on your part. This is because most majors tend to lean, by their very own nature, toward one side or the other—providing students with exciting career-related opportunities or stimulating intellectual growth, which may or may not necessarily lead toward better career opportunities. Fortunately, while career-oriented majors are usually rewarding intellectually, it is also possible to make a liberal arts major even more appealing to prospective employers. However, it will take plenty of your determination, motivation, organization, and planning to accomplish this latter goal. I will have even more to say about this topic in a future chapter when I discuss how you can gain work skills while in college. As you saw in chapter 2, it is especially important to keep your last year in college open for independent study work within your major. This alone will greatly increase your chances for finding satisfying employment after graduation.

Now that you are much more familiar with the structure and functions of college majors, I would like to switch gears for just a bit. I want to help you ask the right questions, which will then lead you to discover a major you are happy and satisfied with.

In defining the self, most people will immediately respond by citing special interests or abilities that characterize them as a unique individual. Choosing a major is much like answering the "Who am I?" question because your answers do not even have to include strictly academically related interests. The next step in how to choose a compatible major is to define your interests. You need to define all of your interests, or at least as many as you can remember. Such interests might include art talent, musical ability, athletic prowess, or an interest in politics.

## STEP 2: WRITE DOWN AS MANY OF YOUR INTERESTS AS YOU CAN

In order to help you get started, let me share with you how I came up with my own "Who am I?" list. Remember to include both academically and nonacademically related interests, because many nonacademically related interests could turn out to be directly compatible with a major. My main interests include helping other people, reading, writing, artwork, and traveling. These interests culminated into my eventual choice of a major in psychology. In choosing your own major, it is very important that you make out a list and rank your interests in order of their importance, or weigh them appropriately. You may find the weighting scale shown in appendix A to be helpful in this regard.

## STEP 3: RANK YOUR INTERESTS IN ORDER OF THEIR IMPORTANCE

Why did I not choose art as my major, or perhaps business, for my enjoyment of travel? Simple. First, I ranked my interests in order of their importance to me. Helping other people ranked the highest on my list of interests. Art and travel fell more toward the middle. Then, I weighted each of my interests, using the scale shown in appendix A.

Writing down the many interests you might have, even some that might seem trivial or unimportant at first glance, is vitally important in helping you to discover a compatible major. Try not to limit yourself into thinking, "What can I do for a career with this type of major?" At this point, you should only be writing down your interests.

## STEP 4: LOOK AT DESCRIPTIONS OF MAJORS IN COLLEGE CATALOGS

Another good way of narrowing down choices for a compatible major is by scanning through college catalogs, preferably that of your own school or the one you plan on attending. Take a look at the descriptions of the majors within the catalog. This will help you to decide if your academic or intellectual strengths match that of a given major. Sometimes, catalog descriptions by themselves will help you to reach a decision about whether or not a major would suit your academic interests and personality. At the very least, using this strategy may help you to eliminate some undesirable choices. It may also help if you read over several versions of the same major. Between catalogs, the same major might sound very different indeed.

It pays to be flexible when choosing your major. Never underestimate yourself or your abilities while thinking about a potential major. However, if you have read through a description of a major that sounds completely opposite to your interests or talents, chances are good that particular major may not be best suited to meet your needs at this point. On the other hand, it is very important for you to keep your interests and abilities in mind while scanning through the catalogs. Used in combination, these two methods will give you the strongest and most likely chance of discovering your ideal major. Either method used alone is a lot less successful in helping you discover how your interests best match up to a major.

## STEP 5: MAKE A DECISION

Making lists of your interests, abilities, and other academic needs, as well as scanning through college catalogs, is vital to your success in finding a suitable major the first time around. While it is very important to have confidence in your own intuitive ability to choose a compatible major, never neglect the opinions of those closest to you. In the end, though, the final decision should be yours and yours alone. You are the one who will be putting in the work and effort toward achieving your goal of discovering a compatible major, completing your major requirements, and graduating from college. Try to be firm about your decision regarding your choice of a major. Take the process of choosing a major seriously, so that you will not be forced to change to another major. Put as much thought as you can into reaching an intelligent and carefully planned decision. Write down all important thoughts and questions you have regarding particular majors. This way, you will not have to change majors several times, sometimes a long and difficult process in itself, later on during your college career.

I first went about this process in entirely the wrong manner. As you will remember, I was an economics major during my first semester in college. I did not choose this major by serious introspection, or by an analysis of my own needs, interests, abilities, and goals. Instead, I picked that particular major because I thought it would be easy for me. During the fall semester of my senior year in high school, I was required to take a class in economics. It turned out to be a very pleasant surprise. I was not even sure if I knew what economists did, but I felt it could not be too bad of an occupation. I decided to give it a try. Well, you already know the rest of my story. Economics in college, I soon found out, was a lot different than economics in high school. My major in economics lasted only one semester. Unfortunately, my next major lasted even less time than that. Finally, during my third and final time of declaring a major, I got my act together. I made out the lists, scanned through the descriptions of majors in the college catalogs, asked for opinions from those closest to me, and I thought a lot about what I would finally declare as a major. In other words, I took the process seriously the third time around. I engaged in some serious introspection regarding my options of choosing particular majors. However, you do not have to change majors two, three, or even four times before you get it right. You can avoid the mess I went through and get it done right the first time around.

At last I made the decision to major in psychology. It was a decision that saved me from future agony in the whole realm of choosing a major. With hindsight, I now feel that my third and final decision to major in psychology could have been made much earlier. I want to save you from experiencing the same agony I went through in my search for a compatible major. My commitment and dedication to college was present, but my planning certainly was not. You can save yourself future stress and needless anxiety by declaring your major for a first and last time. Plan your major.

# 4

## Transferring: When Enough Is Enough

For those of you already in college, this chapter will be especially important. It will give you a chance to objectively examine the relationship you have with your school. This chapter is also very important for those of you who made a "mistake" in selecting your choice of college the first time around. There is always hope. Here is a typical scenario of a transfer wanna-be:

> It is the end of your first year in college. You are deeply dissatisfied with your college, major, and life. Going to college no longer sounds like an opportunity to gain intellectual growth and development or to further expand your future career opportunities. Instead, college is beginning to look more and more like a four-year prison sentence with an expensive price tag. You are constantly left wondering: Is this what I am really supposed to be getting out of college? Am I really supposed to be here?

Those of you already in college may identify with the above scenario. If so, it may mean several different possibilities:

- You really do need to transfer.
- You need to change or reevaluate your current major.
- You need to start living off campus if you are currently an on-campus resident.
- You need to change or reevaluate your reasons for being in college.

- You may not be objectively weighing the pros and the cons of your college and how it matches your needs—that is, you may not be taking advantage of all that your college has to offer you.
- You need a life.

If, after reviewing these options, you are still adamant about transferring, hang on. While transferring is not nearly as difficult as it is sometimes made out to be, and is considerably easier today than a few decades ago, it will still require substantial commitment, dedication, and planning for you to make a smooth transition between schools. This time, you will have the added pressure of making a better decision than you did the first time around. You will have to make certain your transfer school is compatible with your academic goals and personal interests, as well as your personality. The first thing you will want to do if you are considering transferring is to make a list of the pros and cons of transferring from your current institution to a new school. Appendix D shows an example of such a list.

## STEPS TO SUCCESS

1. Make a list of why you want to transfer.
2. Analyze your relationship with your school.
3. Compare your college's actual vs. ideal qualities.
4. Write down all of the courses you have passed.
5. Try to determine the transferability of classes.
6. Apply as a junior transfer student.
7. Consider transferring from a two-year school.

## STEP 1: MAKE A LIST OF WHY YOU WANT TO TRANSFER

Use at least ten major criteria to substantiate this list. If your pros heavily outweigh your cons by seven in ten or more (70 percent), then you are a serious candidate for transferring. However, your final decision will still be far from complete at this point.

If your list looks anything like mine did during my first year of college, right before I decided to transfer, then you are probably a serious candidate for transferring. Even if our lists are not that similar, a couple of items on my sample list are especially critical in assessing whether or not you are truly unhappy at your present school and do need to move on. These two items include the quality of education you perceive as presently received and a lack of "good feeling" for the college. When I was contemplating transferring, these were two of my grievances. I felt the education I was receiving was inadequate, both within and outside my major. As you probably remember from chapter 1, I did not have a good feeling about the school from the moment I set foot on campus. My other complaints included a change in my political ideology, dislike of the big city, and need for a smaller campus.

## STEP 2: ANALYZE YOUR RELATIONSHIP WITH YOUR SCHOOL

Before you decide to transfer on the basis of your list of complaints, make sure you have been doing your part by trying to make your school a successful place for you to be. If you have not been putting forth the effort to make a nice home at your present college, chances are good the people at your school will make no concerted effort on their own to serve your needs. You should know if you have been doing your part to make this relationship work. Have you been taking responsibility and ownership for your college experience? If it is clearly an asymmetrical relationship and you have been putting forth the effort, while the faculty and staff at your school have done virtually nothing to help you in your time of need, chances are good that the time is right for a change of scenery.

So, have you been doing your fair share in order to make this relationship work? Or have you been putting forth all your effort to succeed and you still feel crummy about being at that particular college? If your answer is "yes" to either of these questions, then it is definitely time for you to move on to better and brighter horizons.

The "when" of deciding to transfer is a much more difficult question to address. In chapter 5, I discuss the formal procedures necessary for smoothly implementing the transfer move itself. Now, paperwork procedures aside, I would like to help you decide, should you determine that you want and need to transfer, when the time will be right for you to start thinking about making the move.

Basically, anytime after your first quarter or semester in college, the time will be right, not necessarily to transfer but for you to conduct an honest evaluation of how your college has or has not yet met your needs and expectations. By the end of my first semester as a freshman, I knew that my own campus had not yet met my needs and expectations. However, since I did not make a list of what exactly was not being met, I was not able to narrow down the problem. It was not until a year later that I was able to prepare a list of complaints of how my school was not meeting my ideal college standards. This is an advantage you obviously can have right now.

## STEP 3: COMPARE YOUR COLLEGE'S ACTUAL VS. IDEAL QUALITIES

First of all, start by comparing your present college's qualities, as you currently perceive them, to your ideal college qualities, as described in chapter 1. How satisfied are you between these two lists? Have the gaps narrowed or widened during your first few months in college? This should be your ultimate test in deciding whether or not you should finalize the decision to transfer.

The initial measurements and self-reflection needed to manage a successful transfer move should ideally be made during your first year of college. By the end of your first year of discontentment, you should be able to begin the planning phases of your transfer. The summer after your first year in college, or preferably during winter break, if you are that determined about transferring, write down all the classes you have taken at your current school. At this point, it helps if you know what you would like to major in. This is because most colleges require transfer students to have already declared a major upon entrance to their school. Most schools also require students to complete the necessary lower-division requirements within their major. Some colleges may even mandate students to complete all of their general education requirements before transferring.

## STEP 4: WRITE DOWN ALL OF
## THE COURSES YOU HAVE PASSED

You should start working on this list soon after you have completed your first year in college. Write down all of the courses you have passed that year. Be sure and include them even if you have questions regarding their transferability. With this list in your hands, you will be ready to zoom down to your local college, the public library, or the Internet and check out the college catalogs of your prospective transfer schools. Open each of these catalogs to the pages listing college administration offices, preferably including the office of admissions. Write a formal letter to the office of admissions at each of your prospective transfer schools. In this letter, express your sincere interest in attending their college as a transfer student. Ask the office of admissions to send you information on the school in general, your major or prospective major, and an application for admission. Appendix E shows a sample letter written to the office of admissions.

After your letters are safely in the mail, your work is far from being over. With your list of classes in hand, you will need to decide whether or not you will be able to find comparable lists of classes at the schools where you are considering transferring. You can do this by searching through the college catalogs. When you are looking to find comparable lists of classes, make sure that you thoroughly read through the course descriptions, not merely the course titles. Most schools that accept transfer students are considerate when it comes to letting you know about the policies at their institution regarding transfer credit. In their response letters, schools will generally let you know about such policies. Be aware that some colleges and universities have a more liberal transfer credit policy than others. This may very well be a crucial factor in your decision of whether or not to attend a particular school.

## STEP 5: TRY TO DETERMINE THE TRANSFERABILITY OF CLASSES

When you browse through the college catalogs, try to find classes that are similar to the ones you have already taken. Such classes will probably be

your equivalent "transfer credit"—a word you will be hearing a lot of until graduation.

## STEP 6: APPLY AS A JUNIOR TRANSFER STUDENT

Does the question of "when" to transfer still plague your mind? It certainly should! Unfortunately, while there are no "right" times to transfer,
there are, paradoxically, "wrong" times. There are also ideal times in
which to transfer. Some colleges will accept first-year transfer students;
most will not. Few colleges, with the big exception of two-year junior and
community colleges, will ever accept transfer students who are still in
their first year of college. Ideally, colleges will look for what they call
"junior transfer" students. These transfer candidates have already completed two years of college course work and will be juniors upon entering
their new school. Generally speaking, junior transfers have the best
chance of being accepted, since colleges are looking for transfer students
who can begin completing their upper-division major requirements.

Usually, junior transfers will need to apply in the fall of their sophomore
year in college. However, this can vary substantially, as some colleges have
deadlines as late as May. Since you will probably have a year left at your
old school, you will need to make sure you have decided what classes will
transfer to your future transfer school. Take as many of these transferable
courses as possible during your second year in college. If possible, try and
also complete the lower-division requirements for your major, along with
the general education requirements of your transfer school. This sometimes
helps to increase your chances of being accepted at your first-choice college or university. Above all, try and do as well as possible in all your
courses! Most personnel at college admissions offices will apply the most
weight to your college grades when considering your transfer application.
High school grades are not even glanced at for transfer applicants.

## STEP 7: CONSIDER TRANSFERRING
## FROM A TWO-YEAR SCHOOL

"But I can't stand it here for another day, let alone another year!" Or, "I
don't know yet what I'm looking for in a college. I need another year to find

myself and to discover who I am and where my interests happen to be." Or, "I've heard that it's nearly impossible to transfer from State University A to Prestigious University B." For those of you with these and other similar types of questions, this next section will be especially helpful to you. The two-year junior and community college system can be extremely useful as a means of transferring to a four-year college or university.

Two-year junior and community colleges were founded mostly in the 1950s and 1960s. Their mission: helping the general public gain greater, unrestricted access to higher education. In the 1980s and 1990s, two-year schools were increasingly being used, not only as ends in themselves, but rather as transitional institutions. Students started using two-year colleges as places where they could transfer more smoothly to four-year colleges and universities. Most two-year schools provide a very solid general education. Today, almost all four-year schools recognize the high quality of these types of two-year programs. As a result, many four-year schools now offer what are called transfer articulation agreements with two-year colleges. These transfer articulation agreements all but guarantee admission to top-choice four-year colleges and universities.

For many years now, most two-year colleges have signed transfer articulation agreements with some well-respected four-year colleges and universities—both public and private institutions. These transfer articulation agreements usually specify that if a student makes a certain grade point average (usually a 3.0 or higher), along with completing specific course requirements, both general education and in the intended major, the student will automatically be admitted to the four-year school.

Two-year junior and community colleges may be the perfect answer to all of the concerns addressed earlier. They will:

- Allow you to transfer mid-year.
- Help you discover where your interests are at a low cost, without pressuring you to prematurely declare a major.
- Make the entire process of transferring to a four-year school smoother.

Transfer articulation agreements all but guarantee your admission to a four-year college or university—provided you complete a specific set of courses and obtain a certain grade point average.

# 5

## Transferring: Diving In

In chapter 4, we examined how and when you should decide to transfer from your present college or university to a new school. In this chapter, we explore the formal procedures necessary for you to complete the transfer move. In particular, we focus on transferring from two-year schools to four-year colleges and universities. We also look at two areas that are absolutely essential in any successful transfer move:

- Planning your academic curriculum.
- The actual procedures necessary for starting the transfer application process.

Showing a strong course curriculum from your high school was important if you applied to college right out of high school. As a college transfer applicant, it will be more important for you to show personnel at college admissions offices that you have taken serious and demanding course work during your first two years in college. Along with your grades, the types of college classes you have taken, or plan on taking, will be heavily weighted in your admission prospects as a transfer student. In chapter 5, we explore what types of classes are good, transferable courses for you to consider taking. In addition, I will also help you in deciding when you might want to take certain classes to ensure a faster and more efficient transfer. Throughout this chapter, I will be emphasizing why it is vitally important for you to plan an academic program for the remainder of your first two years at your present school.

## STEPS TO SUCCESS

1. Plan a two-year academic program.
2. Complete college general education requirements.
3. Visit the transfer center at your two-year college.
4. Make an appointment to see an academic advisor.
5. Begin your essay early.
6. "Sell yourself" in your essay.

## STEP 1: PLAN A TWO-YEAR ACADEMIC PROGRAM

What are some "good" courses you should plan on taking? While I obviously cannot present a list here that would suit all readers, I recommend two strategies you can use to pick out "good" classes and solidify the rest of your academic program.

First, plan on fulfilling all of the lower-division course requirements within your major. Of course, try to do as well as possible in these classes. Keep in mind that although some schools will allow you to complete certain lower-division requirements after you transfer, most schools will frown on students trying to fulfill class requirements that really should have been completed during the first two years of college.

Second, although one or two upper-division courses within your own major can sometimes be a plus for a transfer applicant, indicating a serious interest in the major, there are also a couple of flaws in this line of thinking. One flaw is that upper-division coursework of any kind can sometimes be difficult to transfer. Another catch is that personnel in charge of making admissions decisions may be led to the conclusion that you are unnecessarily sacrificing your liberal arts general education in favor of a premature commitment to a major.

So, what are some "good" classes you should consider taking? As a general rule, most introductory general education courses in the liberal arts are respected among personnel in admissions offices. Classes in topics such as underwater basket weaving, kite flying, or bowling, as well as any type of remedial coursework, will not necessarily hurt your application—but these types of classes will not help your cause either!

Remember, while it is advisable to complete your lower-level major course requirements before transferring, it is also very important to remember that most schools will not accept you as a transfer student without your first completing most, if not all, general education requirements.

## STEP 2: COMPLETE COLLEGE GENERAL EDUCATION REQUIREMENTS

Checking on your general education requirements should ideally be done as soon as possible after you have made your decision to transfer. Check the college catalog of your prospective transfer school for details regarding general education requirements. Generally, for those of you planning on transferring between two four-year institutions, you should plan on checking out what the transfer policy is at your prospective transfer school. This can be done by looking at the section of the college catalog under the title "Transfers" or "Transfer Students." It is also important for you to write a formal letter to the office of admissions at your prospective transfer school. A sample letter written to the office of admissions is shown in appendix E. In this letter, ask them to send you information regarding their transfer credit policy. Oftentimes, college catalogs by themselves will not give you all the details needed in order for you to completely understand their particular transfer credit policy.

If possible, it is an excellent idea for you to meet with staff or faculty who specialize in helping new transfer students. A meeting such as this will almost certainly bring you more valuable information and insight than a college catalog or a letter by itself ever will. Obviously, using all three strategies would all but guarantee you the strongest possible information. Most colleges are unique in their acceptance policies of transfer students and they accept at least a small percentage of transfer applicants—so a visit to your local college or public library is a must.

The picture for two-year junior and community colleges is quite a bit different. Here, it is easier to make a constructive, generalized statement regarding what the transfer process usually involves. It usually involves either a procedure similar to transferring between two four-year schools, or a transfer articulation agreement, as mentioned briefly in chapter 4. As you will recall, the transfer articulation agreement is a specified contract that all but guarantees your admission to a four-year college or university. The basic requirements of these contracts are that you first meet minimum academic criteria at your two-year college, such as by maintaining a certain grade point average and taking specific types of courses. By signing a transfer articulation agreement with a campus of the University of California and my local two-year community college, I was able to easily transfer to this first-choice school during my junior year in college.

Should you decide to transfer from a two-year junior or community college to a four-year college or university, you should make an appointment to meet with an academic advisor at the beginning of your sophomore year in college. Both of you will plan the remainder of your second-year course curriculum. Since your advisor may know which courses will transfer, you will be able to plan on taking classes that will directly boost your chances of transferring. These courses will be written down on a contract and a copy will then be sent to your prospective transfer school. Your prospective transfer school will then return another copy to you or your advisor, with approval or denial of the transfer articulation agreement. Provided you have met the course and grade point average requirements specified in the contract, you will automatically be admitted to the transfer school following completion of the specific requirements. Of course, you will still be required to complete the application for admission, but this process will be just a formality at this point.

At this point, I cannot emphasize enough the importance of choosing a good academic advisor in helping you during the planning phases of your transfer. I would highly recommend that you do not randomly pick out an advisor. I can almost guarantee you that this will not work, unless you are very lucky. Get to know your advisor. One good way to find a competent and knowledgeable academic advisor is to ask around on your campus. Ask other students at your college who is highly regarded. In my case, I did not ask—at first. When I went to see my first academic advisor at my two-year community college during my sophomore year in college, I was absolutely adamant about transferring—but I was told I had plenty of time to plan for my transfer. Not liking this advice at all, I went to see another advisor.

As it turned out, my next advisor informed me that I could and should transfer during the upcoming fall term and that I should start planning for the transfer right away. Grateful for this advice, along with a practical plan of how to achieve this goal, I transferred during the fall of my junior year. As it turned out, I ended up graduating from college less than two years later, a whole two terms ahead of schedule! Had I taken the first piece of advice, which happened to be advice I instantly did not like or feel comfortable with, it probably would have taken me six years to graduate. I might never have transferred schools. By the way, transferring turned out to be a move that proved in time to be wonderfully wise. What a difference good planning and a good academic advisor can make!

## STEP 3: VISIT THE TRANSFER CENTER
## AT YOUR TWO-YEAR COLLEGE

Most two-year junior and community colleges have a transfer center. The first thing you will want to do, if you are considering taking this route, is to go to the transfer center at your local junior or community college. While there, ask about any programs that exist to aid transfer students. You will almost certainly be made aware of any automatic transfer admissions policies that exist at your local two-year school, especially if it is a public two-year junior or community college, such as the transfer articulation agreement discussed earlier.

While visiting the transfer center, be sure to specifically ask about services that might be available to help students who want to transfer to four-year colleges and universities. If possible, sign a transfer articulation agreement between your current two-year junior or community college and your four-year prospective transfer school.

## STEP 4: MAKE AN APPOINTMENT
## TO SEE AN ACADEMIC ADVISOR

After you have chosen your prospective transfer school (you may wish to refer to chapter 1 on how to choose your ideal school), be sure and make an appointment with a competent academic advisor. Both of you will need to discuss your plans on transferring. More than likely, if your present college does not have a transfer articulation agreement with the school you would like to attend, then your advisor will probably suggest that you write a letter to the school for more information. Your advisor may even suggest that you look in the library or on the Internet for further information on transferring.

In the event you are able to find an ideal transfer school that has a transfer articulation agreement with your present two-year college, then you will be in great luck. In this case, while your path will still require much work, the entire planning process will be taken care of in a matter of a few meetings with your academic advisor.

Still, after the paperwork for your transfer articulation agreement has been filled out and turned in, your work is far from being over. In fact, it has only just begun! Oftentimes, the motivation to do well in college can be very difficult when classes get especially tough. Most transfer articulation agreements do not let you get away with taking "easy" classes for admission into their four-year colleges and universities. Throughout this book, I have implied that motivation is a strong element of your success in college. Motivation is one of the qualities you will need to continually nurture, should you decide to transfer.

After you have decided to transfer, and even after you know what classes you will need to be taking, you will still need to fulfill perhaps the most difficult part of the contract, and the one that often catches many students completely off guard. You will need to not only pass your classes but you will also need to do very well in them. In the meantime, you should be constantly reminding yourself that you will be achieving the reward of going to a more compatible school when you have successfully completed your contract requirements. Since you are already in college, you are certainly bright and motivated, and aware of the challenges inherent in achieving a college education. If you cannot gather the motivation or energy needed to do well in your courses, it is important to ask yourself if you will really have the motivation and energy that are essential for success at your new school.

I realize none of this is easy, just as most worthwhile things in life never come easily. But at least the planning phase will be taken care of, and that is a huge step to begin with—you know exactly what you need to take next quarter or semester. This knowledge is one of the greatest benefits in signing a transfer articulation agreement.

## STEP 5: BEGIN YOUR ESSAY EARLY

Suppose you are not able to sign a transfer articulation agreement. Then what? Do you still have a chance to go to an ideal college or university? You certainly do have this opportunity, but the essay you write for your transfer application will now become very important. You will usually apply as a transfer student during the fall of the year before you wish to transfer. During August or September of that year, pick up the application forms from your prospective transfer schools and read them over. Think about how you are going to fill out these forms. However, do not write down a thing on the applications—at least, not yet. Look over the essay portion—how are you going to answer it? My best advice to you is to start working on your essay well in advance—at least two months prior to the application deadline. This will allow you plenty of time for rewrites as well. One month before the deadline, you can begin writing rough drafts of your applications on other sheets of paper. In fact, it is a very good idea to photocopy the applications so you can use these copies as "rough drafts" of the applications—without prematurely putting down things on the applications you might want to think about first, before turning in your final versions. Within a few weeks of the deadline, your essays should be finished, or very nearly finished. Write a rough draft of your classes and activities on other sheets of paper. Only after the information has been checked for errors and accuracy should you even begin to touch the original applications themselves.

Writing a good essay is critical in your admission to a four-year college or university if you are directly transferring between two four-year schools. How can you go about writing a good essay? As I have already said, allow yourself plenty of time to write a good essay. Very few masterpieces have ever been written overnight, and college application essays are certainly no exception. Rome was not built in a day—and good final versions of college admission essays are never written in one day or night, either. If you have allowed yourself at least two months in advance of the deadline in order to write your essay, you will not be panic-stricken when the deadline approaches. Be sure to visit your college or local public library. Look for good books designed to help you write better essays. There are plenty of them out there and new ones are coming to bookstores virtually every day. Check them out, take them home, and write down any helpful hints you find as you read these books.

Most colleges and universities have a writing center, or at least a writing lab, where students can get help with their papers. Take advantage of this very valuable resource while you are drafting your college essays! The bottom line: you will want to do a good job on the essay portion of the application, especially if you have not signed a transfer articulation agreement. Most schools are unwilling to admit anyone, especially a prospective transfer student, with poor writing ability and a lack of constructive, critical thinking skills. Your essay can help demonstrate these skills to admissions personnel.

### STEP 6: "SELL YOURSELF" IN YOUR ESSAY

Colleges and universities are going to be looking at how you have matured during your first two years in college. In other words, they are going to be looking at you much differently than they would be viewing a prospective first-year college student who is still unproven in a college environment. The best way to use this fact to your advantage is to "sell yourself" to the admissions personnel. Usually, the essay question or topic will be broad enough to allow you the flexibility and opportunity to include your major accomplishments, dreams, and goals. Now is the time and place to use them constructively. However, at the same time, never drone on about yourself excessively or become overly pretentious about your abilities and accomplishments—this can be very dangerous. If you answer the question honestly, then by all means, go and display your strong qualities in your essay.

An assertive and confident yet subtly modest tone will add a definite spark to your essay. For example, words such as "strong will" and "determined" are both components of an assertively written essay. Also, be sure and include all relevant jobs and activities in your essay. Do not even think of mentioning high school—unless you accomplished something truly exceptional there, such as being class valedictorian, and you can somehow link it on to your present experience in college.

In the midst of your planning and writing, never neglect the most important thing of all, the due dates of your applications! At least two weeks prior to the due date for each application, you should have completed your entire application packet. Remember to enclose your essay and the application fee for each application. It is a good idea to send your application via certified or registered mail, particularly if you are mailing your application close to the deadline. Usually, most schools will send you a postcard or a letter upon receipt of your application, just to confirm they have received your application and will be in the process of reviewing it. Never call the admissions offices directly to find out whether or not you have been admitted, unless a school has already announced that all candidates would be hearing from them by a certain date, and you still have not heard any news.

If you apply in late fall, do not expect to be hearing from the admissions offices until at least early the following spring, in March or April. Most schools have a deadline of April or May, when they will begin sending out acceptance and rejection letters to students. Some schools send these notices out quite early (I once received an acceptance letter in late January), but this is the exception, rather than the rule. The second time I transferred, to a campus of the University of California, I did not get formally accepted until April of my sophomore year. Be prepared to wait. Most schools will decide on new freshman admissions before new transfer admissions, so it is more than likely you will be the last group to find out the final word. Hopefully, though, the long wait will be well worth it.

# 6

## Gaining Work Experience in College

College will help make you more employable in the future. Regardless of your reasons for attending college, you will eventually need to prepare for the work force of the twenty-first century. While liberal arts programs place much less of an overt emphasis on gaining vocational skills, much of the work you will be doing in any academic program will actually be preparing you for life after your college experience is over. To most of us, this means the world of professional work.

The curricula of vocational and liberal arts programs differ on the surface. However, if you look beneath the surface of liberal arts programs, you will discover the hidden agenda of helping you become more attractive to future employers. This hidden agenda of liberal arts programs includes helping you develop advanced skills in reading, writing, critical thinking, and oral communication. This chapter helps you explore ways to make the most of your work experience in college

### STEPS TO SUCCESS

1. Visit the career center early on.
2. Check out internship possibilities.
3. Seriously consider doing an internship in college.
4. Become a volunteer.
5. Explore the working world.

and to enhance your future chances for achieving successful, suitable, and lasting employment.

## STEP 1: VISIT THE CAREER CENTER EARLY ON

Most colleges and universities have job placement agencies and career centers. The first thing you will want to do during your first two years in college will be to visit the career center at your school. Most colleges now have at least one such office, and if your college does not, you can most likely find a nearby institution that does have one. Job placement agencies and career centers are often located either in the same building or they are very close to one another. You will probably want to find information from the staff at these centers on how to properly use their resources. Knowing how to look up information and also knowing where it is located will end up saving you a great deal of time. Career centers and job placement agencies differ greatly between colleges. If you are a transfer student, or if you are considering transferring, you may want to visit the career center of your prospective transfer school. Usually, visitors can browse through the materials in these facilities, although there is sometimes a nominal fee for using these resources.

Career centers often become overcrowded with students late in the spring semester, so the best time to visit the career center is probably either in the summer or fall. There is usually a rush of panic-stricken seniors during April and May, when these students suddenly decide they had better get some information on career opportunities after they leave college. However, you can certainly avoid this mess by going to the career center as early as possible during the school year. You can never be too early in your visit to the career center.

## STEP 2: CHECK OUT INTERNSHIP POSSIBILITIES

During your visit, check to see what the current job openings are for students in your major, especially for people with a bachelor's degree. Also, check to see if there are any related internships in your major for current students. Usually, there are at least a few of them available, and sometimes, these internships even offer monetary compensation or college course credit. Internship experiences also look great on your resume. You should be updating your resume frequently or in the process of creating one. Appendix F shows versions of sample resumes for a current college student and a recent college graduate.

While at the career center, be sure to ask the staff for help in finding out detailed information regarding specific internships. Also be sure to write down any relevant information you find on internships or job openings. Try not to rely on your memory for remembering such important information! Take note of the deadlines for applying for certain internships, and then write down all the information on the relevant internships you find. Check the requirements for internship applicants, the duration or time length of the internships, what you will be doing in these internships, and, of course, the deadlines for your applications.

## STEP 3: SERIOUSLY CONSIDER DOING AN INTERNSHIP IN COLLEGE

Because it is never too early to consider career possibilities, you should seriously consider working as an intern, volunteering, or even doing both during college. This will not only increase your future chances of gaining experience and moving up in your respective field but it will also allow you to finally decide whether or not you really want to enter that career field. Ask around at your school and find out if there are any internships or volunteer experiences that are particularly worthwhile to pursue.

Explain your situation to the staff at the career center. Let them know you are a student at the school and you would like to know more about opportunities for internships, volunteering, or jobs in a field closely related to your major. What interests you? If you are not quite sure yet, be sure to ask the staff at your career center on campus if they have any information on liberal arts internships. Very often, they will have tons of useful information on such opportunities.

## STEP 4: BECOME A VOLUNTEER

Guess how I was able to break into my career as an academic advisor? Yes, as an intern. Granted, I first needed to prepare myself with a couple of years of additional schooling after completing the bachelor's degree. But I can safely say I would not have had the position I did had I not completed an internship first.

While at the career center, be sure to ask about volunteer opportunities. Some people may groan at the very mention of volunteering, but in reality, volunteers often do very productive, worthwhile, and meaningful work. Volunteers are usually not committed to continue working for long, extended periods of time, unlike other workers. Usually, you will be able to find out about volunteer positions related to your major, right along with the internship files.

Volunteer organizations range from names you have probably never heard of before to much more familiar organizations. Volunteers serve in rural environments in the middle of nowhere, urban areas, and just about every place in between. They serve in all areas throughout the United States and the world. Volunteers may be committed to work for a couple of hours or up to several years. Some volunteer opportunities are paid positions, but most are not. The varieties of volunteer activities are simply endless. It is always a good idea to consider checking out the resources at your local college, public library, or the Internet for information on volunteering. Libraries will have tons of useful information on volunteer opportunities, as should many college career centers.

## STEP 5: EXPLORE THE WORKING WORLD

If all else fails, and you cannot seem to find suitable work experience from your school's career or employment office, then you may wish to consider going outside to the world of work. You will need to be very selective, though, in the places you look for work. Contrary to popular belief, it is possible for college students to find work in very satisfying, meaningful positions outside the realm of fast food restaurants and retail clothing stores. In addition to your work experience, your college degree will be a tremendous asset in helping you find stimulating employment after graduation.

When you are still in college, it is partly true that you may have to settle for entry-level, clerical-type positions for the time being. However, you can still gain excellent job skills from such experiences. For example, if you want to work for a marketing agency while in college, then you may need to answer the phones, work more intensively at office tasks, and perform other types of "grunt" work. However, such work experience will be invaluable in helping you to gain expertise within that organization and gives you a chance to move up into more exciting positions later on.

Temporary employment is not just for people who are down on their luck and looking for any job. These opportunities can also help you gain valuable work experience. Open up the yellow pages of your telephone book and look under "Employment—Temporary." There, you will find a listing of all the temporary employment agencies in your area. These placement agencies can help direct you towards the types of organizations where you would like to work.

"Why," you may be asking, "should I go through the trouble of trying to find a good job now? My job is being a college student." Well, that is certainly true, but you will have to eventually start somewhere in the world of professional work, and it really helps to start while you are still in college. Even a year of meaningful work experience will greatly enhance your chances of landing a good job right out of college—alongside your freshly minted college diploma. This will probably also augment your salary as well, putting you, and not just your future employer, in the driver's seat.

During my entire time as a college student, not once did I work for an employment agency or in a professional business setting. Looking back now, I am completely dismayed by my naïve thinking back then. I thought that employers would quickly snatch me up just because I had a college degree! Sure, I worked at jobs, but they were only those—jobs, mostly in retail establishments, grocers, and in the restaurant industry. I knew I did not want to work in these types of organizations after graduating from college, but I took these jobs solely as an easy way to make money. This was a big mistake on my part. My employment experiences during college did not teach me any business-related skills, such as knowledge of computer software programs. They did not even teach me how to type. They also did not teach me how the world of professional business works. In many ways, I was incredibly naïve right out of college, insofar as the world of work was concerned.

One day, after I had recently graduated from college, and was looking for my first full-time professional position, my interviewer told me I would not have very much flexibility in negotiating my salary. This was because I did not have any experience working in professional businesses outside the realm of retail establishments, grocers, and the restaurant industry. The interviewer also told me that college students often come to employment agencies after completing their first year in college, in order to start their professional training. They end up learning many valuable skills during the next three or four years so that, by the time they have graduated from college, they have a substantial say in negotiating their desired salary. In addition, they have also picked up tremendous skills that are helping them out already—fresh out of college. For all practical purposes, my recent college degree by itself seemed to have about as much value as a person just starting out in college. This was a very frustrating experience for me. Undoubtedly, I was upset and disappointed by this rather harsh dose of reality. I want to save you from the heartache I experienced in the world of work.

Fortunately, your college degree can look even better if you can supplement it with professional work experience. Employers will look at college credentials, but usually only as a passing acknowledgment of a general intellectual competency. Having professional skills and experience says a lot to employers—it says you have taken the time to go above and beyond the person who has completed college without having had these same valuable experiences. You will stand out among other job applicants. You will be noticed. You will have more attractive career choices available to you in the future.

Most colleges and universities have a "hidden curriculum" in their course offerings. Sure, one of the purposes of college is achieving intellectual growth, but by the very nature of the college experience, your college education will also help you prepare for the world of work. Researching for a term paper is training for work. So is taking a foreign language class. So is taking a psychology course. My point here is that college does and will inevitably train you for the world of work. However, some of the curriculum in colleges will look more overtly attractive to certain future employers than others. While you can and certainly should supplement a liberal arts education with courses in certain vocations, you should also be made aware that the primary work-oriented purpose of a liberal arts education is helping you gain advanced reading, writing, research, oral communication, and critical thinking skills. While these skills look great on a resume or job application, in addition to these qualities, most organizations today are looking for what they term "directly marketable skills." These are skills in areas such as computer software usage, typing, and oral presentation.

Make no mistake about it: your liberal arts education is a very valuable asset in the world of work. At the same time, however, you should also seriously consider learning professional work-related skills while still in college. This will tremendously boost your career value and attractiveness to employers upon your graduation from college.

# 7

---

## Independent Study Courses and Projects

In chapter 6, I offered you a glimpse of the independent study projects you can do while still in college. In this chapter, we explore in more substantial depth the steps you need to take in order for you to get the most out of your college's academic offerings. In this chapter, we focus on two types of independent study projects: first, we examine research projects and then we look at teaching assistant positions.

### STEPS TO SUCCESS

1. Learn about independent study projects.
2. Explore research project opportunities.
3. Know how much time you will spend on the project.
4. Ask about your duties.
5. Explore research assistant positions.
6. Explore teaching assistant positions.

### STEP 1: LEARN ABOUT INDEPENDENT STUDY PROJECTS

For most of you, taking classes at your college probably has become, or will soon become, "old hat." Colleges and universities have a lot more to offer you, however, than just plain lecture classes. If you look inside your college catalog, or almost any college catalog for that matter, you will find listed inside a number of independent study projects within your own major. Most of these projects require you to first complete a number of prerequisites within your major or to have achieved a certain class standing.

One reason why these independent study projects are easier to find than other types of internships is because they are essentially embedded into the academic curriculum of your college or university. In most cases, you can actually sign up for these projects much as you would a normal course. A second reason why this route is generally easier to get started on is because advisors are usually a lot easier to find for these types of courses, because almost all colleges and universities require an advisor or instructor for all of their college courses—including independent study projects listed as courses. Finally, these projects are easier for future graduate school personnel and future employers to investigate what actually went on in these courses. It is more difficult for them to check on projects not listed as courses offered by the college, since most internships and volunteer positions are not under the direct auspices of the school. In other words, most internship and volunteer positions are usually not directly associated with the institution itself. For these and many more reasons, independent study projects offer you a more convenient way for your future employers to analyze the structure of the program and its validity.

Why should you choose to become involved with independent study projects in the first place? Well, for one thing, they look great on graduate school applications, as well as on your resume for future professional employment. They also offer you the convenience of being able to sign up for these projects the same way you would sign up for a regular course. These types of projects also offer you a glimpse of your major that regular courses often seriously lack. You can gain very valuable insight into your major by doing an independent study project.

When I did my first independent study project in psychology, I was exposed to a major that was much more complicated and exciting than I had ever before dreamed possible. If you ask other students who have taken on independent study projects, they will most likely tell you the projects take you to a much higher level, a horizon that cannot be reached simply by taking a lecture course—no matter how difficult that course happens to be. It is much easier to decide on whether or not you would like to enter a career based upon independent study projects, rather than by classes alone.

## STEP 2: EXPLORE RESEARCH PROJECT OPPORTUNITIES

Types of research projects will vary greatly, depending on your major. Almost all majors offer some type of coursework that is devoted almost exclusively to helping you further explore some special topic of interest. These research projects are especially plentiful in the sciences, and many offer you a golden opportunity to see if you would really like to pursue a future career in your major. Be sure to note the requirements necessary in order for you to become involved with such advanced research. Many instructors of these courses require you to have a substantial course background before signing up for these projects. This assures these instructors that you will have a general background from which to begin your work on their projects. I would like to illustrate how I became a research assistant in psychology through the independent study format. Hopefully, my own story will encourage you to go about finding a suitable research position in your own major.

It was the fall of my junior year in college. I was taking my first upper-division class in psychology at my new school. By chance, one day another student told me about the possibilities of working as a research assistant. It turned out that this particular student had been working with a psychology professor and several other students on a research project in social psychology. This student explained the project to me, and shortly afterward, I decided to sign up for the course. For the following year, I would be doing an independent study research project in psychology.

Usually, it is not wise to wait and hope that a person will come along and introduce you to these types of projects. In my case, this is exactly what happened, but it need not be the same case with you. In fact, I would strongly recommend not waiting around! Many colleges and universities post these types of project listings outside or near their department offices. It is a very good idea to check out these projects well in advance, as they are very popular with students, and these spots fill up quickly. If possible, I would recommend that you sign up a quarter/semester or more in advance of when you would like to take these types of courses.

You will almost always be required to attend an interview with the professor in charge of the project before you will be considered for the position. These interviews are usually fairly formal, so dress appropriately and treat it as you would a professional job interview. Remember to express a sincere interest in helping with the project. Most professors will ask you to tell them what you feel you can contribute to their current research. A good answer here is to cite your relevant past and current coursework. Be sure to let the professor know you have a specific interest in exploring their current field of research.

## STEP 3: KNOW HOW MUCH TIME
## YOU WILL SPEND ON THE PROJECT

Once you have signed up, interviewed, and are accepted to register for the course, you will need to plan a working schedule showing how many hours per week you are willing and able to commit to the project. You will also need to plan the times you expect to set aside to work on the project, including time spent in the laboratory. Try to be reasonable in estimating how many hours per week you are willing to commit to the project. When I first enrolled in the independent study research course, I naïvely thought that I would be devoting about twenty-five to thirty hours per week on the project. As it turned out, ten to fifteen hours per week was a far more reasonable estimate.

If possible, try to find out how many hours per week you will be expected to put into the course. It will usually not be worth your time or effort if you are expected to put in more than twenty-five hours per week on the project and are also taking a full load of classes besides. You do not want to let your other classes suffer, even if the project absolutely enraptures you. Also, be sure to find out if there will be a required term paper for the course. As one of the few drawbacks to these types of projects, short term papers are usually a requirement for the course. Before making a final decision committing to the project, add the number of hours you expect to be working on the term paper to the hours you will already be devoting to helping with the research project.

Generally, these types of projects should require anywhere from ten to twenty hours of time committed per week, including time spent on outside research. Again, be sure to check and see how much time you are expected to commit to the project.

## STEP 4: ASK ABOUT YOUR DUTIES

Remember to ask about your duties. Will you be serving coffee and doughnuts to the professor? Will you have a legitimate chance to do some authentic research within your major? How much time will you be allowed to work on the project independently? How much time will require direct supervision?

Be careful when assessing both your overall course workload and your expected project duties. Try to narrow down the exact requirements for successfully completing the project. Do not be afraid to ask the professor or graduate student in charge of the project how much you will actually be contributing to the direct advancement of the research. It might also be a good idea to ask how your future contribution will change or add further strength to the research. In other words, how will your contribution have made a difference?

## STEP 5: EXPLORE RESEARCH ASSISTANT POSITIONS

Not all research positions are offered as courses. In fact, many will not be listed as courses. Professors are often looking for hard-working, dedicated, and committed students to help them with their current research projects. Most of these research positions will be paid. Often, however, it may be quite difficult to get these types of positions since they are not offered as formal courses, and so they will require a lot more initiative on your part in order to find out about these projects. Look for these positions either in the listings for job openings on campus or in the department office of your major. You can also ask your professors directly about any possible job openings in their current line of research.

If you are currently taking a class, or if you have previously taken a class with a professor with whom you might like to work, visit the professor either after class or during office hours. During your meeting, politely ask him or her if there are any available positions for research assistants. Although professors sometimes have more than a few positions open, they usually have only one or no available openings. Unfortunately, there is usually not a whole lot you can do about this either. Paid research positions look great on your resume, but they are generally more difficult to get and will require initiative, motivation, and perseverance on your part to obtain them.

What will you be doing as a research assistant? This question is purposely a very general one, but also an extremely important one to revisit. All majors are unique. So too will your expected duties as a research assistant be unique. As a psychology major, I was expected to attend weekly one-hour meetings, conduct psychology experiments in the laboratory, perform data entry tasks, and look up psychology articles in the library. In the sciences, research positions are usually readily available because the nature of science itself is in doing research. Within the sciences, though, duties of research assistants will range from doing laboratory experiments to library research and reading, as well as writing possible literature reviews on what you have read in the library. Another type of independent study project, which is more difficult for undergraduates to obtain, is a teaching assistant position.

## STEP 6: EXPLORE TEACHING ASSISTANT POSITIONS

Teaching assistants are needed across the board in academia, from biology to history to psychology. The demand is especially prevalent at larger institutions, but even at the largest universities, the possibility of an undergraduate being assigned a teaching assistant position is still quite low—the main reason being the presence of graduate students. Usually, but not always, graduate students are given first priority in teaching assistant assignments, since most of them are required to assist in teaching at least one course, and usually many more, during their graduate school career. As an undergraduate college student, it will be difficult, though it is still sometimes possible, for you to obtain a position as a teaching assistant, either paid or for course credit. If you attend a college where there are no graduate students, then it is possible you might have an easier time finding available teaching assistant positions as an undergraduate.

A few colleges and universities offer courses in being a teaching assistant for specific subjects, and even fewer open these courses to undergraduates. In most cases, if you want to become a teaching assistant, you will have to go directly to the professor of the course you would like to assist teaching. However, this hardly guarantees you a teaching position. Here, I would like to focus on courses geared toward teaching assistant positions. First, we will focus on the duties of the job itself, including its benefits and drawbacks, and what you can expect during your teaching assistantship. Then, we will look at ways you can break into these positions or learn more about possible future openings.

As has been my usual experience, I first learned about the possibilities of becoming a teaching assistant rather passively and by pure chance. During the spring quarter of my junior year in college, I was told there was a course being offered in the fall to seniors called "Teaching College Psychology." I knew it would look great on my application to graduate school, and it would also be a fantastic learning experience so I applied for this position. I was required to submit an essay, and I also had to include a list of the relevant coursework I had taken in my major. In my essay, I mainly discussed my reasons for wanting to become a teaching assistant. I was notified by June that I had been selected for the position. Of course, I was quite elated and jubilant. That summer, I started catching up on reviewing the material for the course I would be assisting in, "Introduction to Psychology." The fall term finally arrived and school started once again. I would have a chance to teach!

Being a teaching assistant is hard, grinding, and demanding work. The duties of most teaching assistants include correcting and grading exams and papers, holding weekly section or lecture meetings, holding office hours, and tutoring your students. Out of these duties, you can expect to spend the majority of your time grading exams and papers, as well as preparing your weekly lessons for class meetings. Be prepared to spend at least ten hours per week grading exams and papers, and up to ten hours per week preparing for your weekly lessons. It is a very good idea to have all of your planning taken care of at least two hours before class starts. This will give you plenty of time to relax, unwind, and think about how you will present the current lesson to the class.

But there is still much more than this simple written description implies. You will have to completely and unconditionally dedicate yourself to the welfare of your students. You will need to be very prepared for the subject you are going to teach. Most of all, you can expect this course to demand a lot of your time, so it is a very good idea to plan what else you will be taking along with this class. If you seriously want to embark on this position, do not carry too many credit hours. You will need most of your free time and energy to dedicate to this position. Many of your weekends will be spent preparing for your discussion sections, along with correcting and grading exams and papers. In a nutshell, these will be your minimal duties. Plan on spending at least twenty to thirty hours per week on this position alone, not including other courses you will also be taking.

The benefits of being a teaching assistant are plentiful. As I mentioned earlier, it will look outstanding on your application to graduate school. It will look great to prospective employers because it shows excellent public speaking abilities and leadership qualities. You can definitely highlight this experience on your professional resume. This experience not only looks good on paper but it also helps you build your self-confidence, self-esteem, and teaching skills. If you plan on becoming a teacher at any level in the future, you should definitely consider applying for a teaching assistant position as an undergraduate, if this opportunity is available to you at your college or university.

The many drawbacks you will find with this job include giving up much of your free time, anxiety and stress over the prospects of first time teaching, and a feeling of deep uncertainty concerning your progress as a teacher. Many weekends will quickly disappear under a huge stack of papers and exams to be graded and lessons to prepare. It is very easy to feel overwhelmed by your duties as a teaching assistant. Only the most highly motivated and energetic of students should apply for this type of position. Usually, your progress will be evaluated only toward the end of the term. With this delayed progress report, it will often be too late for you to change your current teaching style, if needed, during the same term. Fortunately, you will probably be evaluated at the end of the course. You will be able to pick up some important feedback on your teaching from your student evaluations.

Do not expect miracles during your first time as a teaching assistant! Even if you already have outstanding public speaking skills, you can expect to be at least moderately nervous during your first few times on stage. It will eventually wear off, but rather slowly. As I mentioned earlier, your workload will be heavy—but the benefits of these positions far outweigh any negative aspects. There is a feeling of deep personal pride and satis-faction you will experience upon the conclusion of the course, knowing that you have done something very few undergraduates will ever have the opportunity to do: help educate your fellow college students. It will be very difficult for you not to feel intimately involved with your school during this time because you will always be involved at school during your time as a teaching assistant.

# 8

## Completing Your Education within Four Years

This chapter will be helpful if you plan on graduating in four years or less. We will see how and why it may be easier for students in some majors and schools to graduate earlier than others. In this chapter, we also explore how you can sufficiently plan your course curriculum ahead of time in order to minimize your stay in college, regardless of your major. Finally, I share my own story of how I graduated from college in less than four years, along with practical tips on how you can budget your time wisely while still in college.

I have often heard horror stories about students who have taken up to eight years to complete their undergraduate degree as a full-time student. While the school and your major both have a lot to do with promoting this extended period of study, you do have at least some control over how long you plan on staying in school before completing your bachelor's degree. Let me give you a picture of how schools, as well as majors themselves, can lengthen your stay in school unnecessarily.

I have three illustrations of how schools can prolong or shorten your time in college. These pictures derive from my experiences as a student at the California State University, a California community college, and the University of California.

I should also mention here that college characteristics and majors tend to be somewhat interrelated. For example, at most campuses of the California State University, the focus tends to be more on vocational, hands-on training for careers in the "real world." The academic majors at this and other similar types of institutions are therefore fairly traditional, pre-professional, and vocational in nature. At these types of schools, four majors are generally standouts (although, of course, there are many more majors available at these schools): business administration, education, engineering, and nursing. While I do not wish to critique the nature of these majors, I do wish to draw attention to the fact that they are vocational in nature, reflecting the greater preprofessional awareness at these types of institutions.

Most colleges and universities that I dub as being vocational or preprofessional are very much interested in offering you majors that will give you the applied career skills necessary for success in the world of professional work. For example, business administration may help teach you marketing or accounting skills; education will help train you to become a teacher; engineering will give you the background necessary to apply for an entry-level position in the field; and nursing will enable you to obtain a nursing position in a hospital, clinic, or school after you pass the required licensing examination.

While schools that offer more vocational and preprofessional types of majors may very well offer many liberal arts majors, their focus is undoubtedly on training students for the world of professional work. With this extra preparation, the administrators at these schools argue that students should allow plenty of time to complete their major requirements: up to six years of full-time study is the average. However, as I explain later in this chapter, these types of schools will often times drag out all course requirements, including those for liberal arts majors. This is often an attempt by the administrators of these colleges to integrate the "liberal arts" curriculum into an existing curriculum that is primarily vocational and preprofessional in nature. It is a very difficult, and sometimes impractical, challenge to unite both sets of curriculum, the vocational and liberal arts, while still expecting students to graduate within four years. When I examine the curriculum and types of majors found at California State University, you will see why this is, in fact, oftentimes the case.

The University of California, where I completed my undergraduate studies, primarily emphasizes the liberal arts. This is not to say that all campuses of the University of California will neglect the vocations and preprofessional fields. In fact, some of these campuses are well known for their strong curriculum in areas such as engineering and premedical programs. However, the way in which the course curriculum is set up at the University of California, in contrast to the California State University, all but guarantees that most of its students will graduate within four years. In fact, many of the students at the University of California take on two or more majors, internships for course credit, and participate in study abroad programs—and still graduate within four years. The question is: why?

I have come up with two possible answers as to why many students at some types of institutions typically graduate in four years or less. Note that neither reason has anything to do with how "smart" students are at a particular school.

- The liberal arts curriculum is structured more toward having students graduate within four years.
- The quarter system, which is predominantly found on most University of California campuses, is a more suitable calendar system in helping students to complete their education within four years.

Unlike the semester calendar, which is predominantly found on the campuses of the California State University, the quarter calendar found on most University of California campuses may, in fact, help students to more easily complete their bachelor's degree requirements within four years or less. Instead of having two sets of finals during the school year, students who are on the quarter system have three sets. However, by taking fewer classes at a single time, students are also less vulnerable to becoming burned out than while on the semester system.

Regardless of the importance that the academic calendar has on shortening or prolonging students' time in college, I believe that both factors, the academic curriculum and academic calendars, are very important issues. My examples of the California State University and the University of California campuses are not given here because I believe one university system is inherently better than the other. Each system has its own individual strengths and challenges. I share these examples as an explanation for why many full-time students might have different graduation rates based on certain majors and the academic calendar an institution uses. In fact, these are often overlooked factors when we analyze why some school systems have much longer periods of graduation rates than others. It seems odd to me that the calendar system can have that much impact, but I believe it has such an impact because the quarter calendar simply makes planning easier. It also makes goal setting easier when you have to pick out three classes at a time, rather than five or six. It is quite reasonable to speculate that even students with many vocational or preprofessional types of majors offered at their colleges and universities, but whose institutions operate on a quarter calendar, might have faster graduation rates than similar groups of students working under a semester calendar.

Unfortunately, as far as I know, no hard data currently exists to substantiate my claim, but from my own experience, such a possibility seems to be very worthy of future study. While both factors are probably very important, then, the nature of the term system is arguably just as crucial in determining the graduation rates of students at institutions operating under each respective calendar system. When considering a college or university to attend, you may very well wish to examine the type of academic calendar the school operates under. Are you comfortable with such a calendar system? I guarantee that it will have an impact upon such things as planning your course curriculum, balancing your course load with the rest of your life, and being more or less prone to experiencing burnout. It can also impact your plan on graduating from college within a minimum amount of time.

## STEPS TO SUCCESS

1. From day one, plan your course curriculum.
2. Use the guidelines in this book.
3. Never neglect your major's own requirements.
4. Consider enrolling in summer session courses.

## STEP 1: FROM DAY ONE, PLAN YOUR COURSE CURRICULUM

Basically, almost everything you do in college should come down to good planning, as I have been continually emphasizing throughout this book. Semester calendars allow you to become poor planners because of the simple fact that you can only take so many courses during a two-term year, as opposed to a three-term year, and do your very best work in them. Balance is a key consideration here. Students who are taking too many courses, either while on the semester or quarter calendar, may also be less likely to have higher grades than those who are taking fewer courses. The semester calendar, unfortunately, openly encourages students to overload with courses, in order to help compensate for a four-year graduation pace. This can very easily lead to burnout, and in a worst-case scenario, dropping out of college altogether.

The average time it takes a full-time student to receive a bachelor's degree, regardless of major, at the California State University campuses that operate heavily on the semester calendar is five to six years. Many full-time students learning under this calendar system take even longer to graduate, if they end up graduating at all. These facts do not even include nontraditional students, many of whom work many hours and take classes part-time. Again, this is not a critique of this particular university system, but only the academic calendar they choose to operate on. I once calculated, just out of curiosity, that had I not transferred to a University of California campus, which operated on the quarter calendar, it would have taken me at least five years to graduate, in the same major program, with no better of an education. Even if I had taken five courses per semester for four years, I still would not have graduated on time. For me, anyway, that seemed ridiculous. After all, I was a psychology major, not an engineering major! Choice of major, along with the type of academic calendar your school happens to use, seems to be the predominate means of figuring out roughly how long you can expect to be in school as a full-time student.

So what is your major? As you saw in chapters 2 and 3, majors come from all different areas of interest and philosophies. Your own choice of a major will, in part but not entirely, determine how long you can expect to be in college. For example, students in most liberal arts majors will usually graduate closer to four years, while many engineering majors often take one or two years longer to graduate. What is going on here? Is this because liberal arts majors are smarter or better planners than engineering majors? Certainly we know this is not the case! Many engineering majors simply have to fulfill more major requirements than liberal arts students. Even so, I still believe that good planning can help all college students, regardless of their major, graduate within a minimum amount of time.

Type of major only partly determines a student's length of stay in college. The second factor I just mentioned is, of course, the school itself, as well as how you are able to adapt to the academic calendar your school operates on. A final, and perhaps the most crucial determinant of graduating within four years, is your ability to plan your academic curriculum from day one of college. Being able to plan well in advance may help trim one semester, or even one year, off your expected graduation date. The key to graduating in four years or less, or at least in a minimum amount of time, along with achieving most other successes in your college career, is good planning.

Planning from day one is especially important if you plan on graduating in four years or less. Even if you do not know exactly what types of courses you will be taking (or the classes you will need to be taking) your first and second years, most majors in the liberal arts really do not demand a firm commitment to a field of study. Try fulfilling as many of your general education requirements as possible during your first year. Take a wide variety of these types of courses, ranging from writing to science requirements. Check your college catalog to see what you are required to take in the area of general education courses. Plan on deciding on a firm major by the end of your sophomore year. Take a full load of courses, if possible, each and every academic term. See an academic advisor at least once per term, not once per year. All of these actions, along with following the rest of the guidelines in this book, will help you to graduate in the shortest time possible, provided you are willing to put forth the time and effort needed to achieve your academic goals.

## STEP 2: USE THE GUIDELINES IN THIS BOOK

It is necessary to begin writing down your actual plan for graduating within a specific amount of time. In my example, shown in appendix G, I cited four years as my goal for graduation from college. Along with citing the length of time you expect to be in college, it is also necessary to determine course loads per academic term. It is important to list the general education requirements you plan on fulfilling during certain terms. Finally, if you have already made a firm commitment to a major, it is important that you list how many classes will be required in order for you to complete the major, and what classes you will be taking within your program. Write down absolutely every detail. This is not a time for taking "mental notes!" I cannot stress the importance of this enough. I would also suggest that you review your list every term, and make the necessary changes, but try and stick to your original length of college commitment.

The bottom line: it can be done. You can actually plan quite easily. Even if you are currently in college and feel completely stuck in achieving your goal of graduating from college within four years, you can still, at this very moment, plan the remainder of your course curriculum so as to minimize the rest of your time in college. However, this activity does require substantial time, effort, and, most importantly, energy—and lots of it! The planning aspect will help you out tremendously. As you can see from appendix G, I had taken most of my general education requirements during my first two years of college. During my third year, I began fulfilling most of the upper-division requirements in my major, leaving my last year open to take on the independent study projects I described in chapter 7.

Never did I neglect the requirements for my major while fulfilling many campus general education requirements. I took at least one required course in my major beginning from the first semester of my freshman year. By my junior year in college, I only had a few major requirements— all upper-division coursework—left to fulfill. I also had virtually no general education requirements remaining. This is what I mean by effective planning: write down what and when you want to take certain courses to fulfill your academic requirements. Most importantly, however, never neglect one of the most significant parts of your course curriculum, which is your college major.

## STEP 3: NEVER NEGLECT
## YOUR MAJOR'S OWN REQUIREMENTS

Please keep in mind that I was also a transfer student—and yet, I still graduated from college in less than four years. I do not share my story here because I wish to brag. I am certainly no Einstein and I did not study during every waking moment of my life in college. But I was and am an excellent planner. This really helped me achieve my goal of graduating from college in less than four years. With proper planning, you too can quite readily achieve this goal. One of the biggest assets I had was the structure of my own major of psychology. It was a flexible major, so I could basically set my own schedule for when I wanted to complete certain course requirements. For many of you with more structured majors, such as in the vocations and preprofessional fields such as business administration, education, engineering, and nursing, your planning will probably be somewhat easier, since your major department has already developed a plan for the order in which you need to take your classes.

Following from my own example, I used the format I have been generally advocating throughout this book:

- Fulfill as many of your general education requirements as soon as possible.
- Declare a major no later than the end of your sophomore year.
- Consult regularly with a competent professional or faculty advisor.
- Continue fulfilling major requirements beginning from your first quarter or semester in college.

It is very important for you not to neglect the requirements of your own major while you are in the process of fulfilling other university requirements.

## STEP 4: CONSIDER ENROLLING IN SUMMER SESSION COURSES

One of the biggest problems I saw in college was that students were taking much longer than necessary to graduate because they still had a lot of major requirements left to complete during what should have been their last year in college. Taking summer courses can be a helpful way of cutting some of your time off in college. You can often take these classes rather cheaply at your local two-year junior or community college, transfer these classes to a four-year school, and still have time left over to work full-time during the summer or complete an internship. If you take just one summer class per session after each academic year, you can probably cut close to a quarter or semester from your expected graduation date. If you take three or four summer classes each year, you might be able to complete college up to a year earlier. Summer classes usually have less variety than classes offered during the regular school year, but these classes are also usually much smaller in size than those held during the academic year. Definitely consider enrolling in summer session courses. Summer classes will save you a lot of time and money in the future, and so they are a very wise investment.

# 9

## Your Future after College

A college education, despite the occasional frustrations and expense of achieving one, is well worth your effort. Especially for those of you who are nontraditional college students, I feel I do not even have to remind you of the harsh realities of life outside college! In a way, making tough choices during your college career will prepare you very well to face life after college, in a world where you will be making challenging decisions on almost a daily basis. Your future after college will be substantially shaped by the effort you put forth during your time in college. Chapter 9 outlines the final steps in helping you in your quest for future success. In this chapter, we look primarily at how college, and the choices you make during your college experience, will affect your future. The focus of this final chapter is based largely on issues you will be facing after graduation, such as employment and where you will live. We look at the big question many students ask when getting close to graduation: What am I going to do with the rest of my life?

Many recent college graduates often feel somewhat helpless to control their own destinies after the glamour of commencement has long since ended. Recent studies report that only about 25 to 30 percent of all U.S. citizens over age twenty-five hold a bachelor's degree or higher. This means roughly two-thirds to three-fourths of the American adult public did not complete at least the equivalent of a four-year college education. Surely you are among the elite at demonstrating exceptional perseverance, motivation, and commitment. Surely you are now making headway to become an even better planner. Then, why do you feel so much anxiety and uncertainty? Perhaps, you are thinking, the answer is because college does not equal the "real world." This is true, nothing quite equals this jungle, and the possibilities can indeed seem overwhelming at first. However, college has prepared you very well for achieving reasonable success in life after graduation. Be well aware of this irrevocable fact, especially after you have recently graduated from college. It can be a truly rough world out there. Words of encouragement can sometimes be very tough for recent college graduates to come by, particularly in hard economic times. For those of you who are finding your way closer to graduation with every passing day, and yet who are also still stumped and mystified over what to do with your life after college, I would strongly recommend writing down your goals again—your goals after college. I would also like to add these words of encouragement here: there is nothing wrong with "not knowing" what you will do after college. Life is far too complicated to have it all figured out within a matter of a few years, let alone a few decades! First, let us take a look at a couple of basic facts.

## STEPS TO SUCCESS

1. Do not apply to graduate school during college.
2. Create a professional resume.
3. Visit your library or bookstore to brainstorm.
4. Make the decision.

## STEP 1: DO NOT APPLY TO GRADUATE SCHOOL DURING COLLEGE

Two major issues are normally thrust upon most recent college graduates, particularly among "traditional" college students eighteen to twenty-four years of age:

- Whether to seek employment or go immediately on to graduate school.
- Where to live after college.

For most of you, unless you are either really on the ball or are a nontraditional college student, the second question will usually be a little easier to answer than the first. The "whether to" part of the first question can, however, create some major headaches. If you plan on going to graduate school the fall term following your graduation, you will have some serious work and planning ahead of you. Most graduate programs require applicants to submit all their required materials during the fall of the year before they wish to enter their graduate program; in this case, it would mean applying during the fall quarter or semester of your senior year in college. This is by no means an easy task, since with the demands of your current coursework and other commitments, it is often extremely difficult to find time to write your applications and essays and still keep up with your coursework and other commitments on hand. Ask anyone who has applied to graduate school during college what it was like, and you will most likely receive the answer that it was a horrible experience. I strongly discourage you from applying to graduate school while still in college, unless you are an extremely motivated individual. Otherwise, you are very likely to become burned out halfway through the application process.

Since I have no experience of applying to graduate school while still in college, and instead waited until I was out of college for two years before applying, I have received this information from several of my former classmates. I have relied on the accuracy of their reports at face value. However, I might add here, on a personal note, that graduate school applicants do look awfully tired throughout this laborious process. From what I have heard, if you are planning on applying to graduate school while still in college, then plan on giving up a lot of your life at the moment—you simply will not have the time.

So, if you have decided not to risk applying to graduate school right away, should you go ahead and enter the workforce after graduation? Should you travel, or do something unusual and exciting for a change? Or should you commit yourself to a long-term volunteer position? All of these opportunities, and perhaps many more, are at your hands should you decide not to go immediately into a graduate school program. So, the answer to all three of these questions can be "yes." However, additional explanations are also necessary. We will look briefly at opportunities in the workforce, travel, and volunteering, and then I will help you to intelligently take advantage of these opportunities.

Deciding to become a full-time employee should always be seen as a serious commitment, but even more so as a recent college graduate. This is because you will want to know what you are getting yourself into in this type of permanent position. You will also want to make a good start in your first professional position after college. When you first walk into a company, in order to ask about job openings, the first question you will probably be asked is, "So, what type of work are you looking for?" Especially at large, diverse organizations, this question will almost always be asked. Be prepared for it! Do you have an intelligent answer? You should, before you decide to apply. Remember, your first position out of college will probably not be your last one, but it will help to launch you into your career path and possibly even your lifestyle. It is very important not to take this commitment too lightly. One of the first items you will need to create after graduation, regardless of whether or not you intend to become a full-time employee right away, is a professional resume.

## STEP 2: CREATE A PROFESSIONAL RESUME

Your resume is simply a personalized professional document that lists your educational background, skills, experience, and employment history. The Internet, the public library, and your own college library have many good books on how to create a resume and cover letter, so it is important to pay a visit to your local library before you start working on your resume. Since there are many useful books out there targeted for recent college graduates searching for jobs, I will only add here that the best cover letters and resumes are usually the ones that will get the interviews. Therefore, your chances of being hired will actually increase the better you look on paper, as well as in person. Unless you have an outstanding work history, be sure to mention your educational credentials toward the top of the resume page. You may wish to review appendix F. The second resume shown is a sample for a recent college graduate. Note the differences in the ordering of items, as well as the content, for a current college student's resume versus a resume for a recent college graduate.

## STEP 3: VISIT YOUR LIBRARY OR BOOKSTORE TO BRAINSTORM

If you are less than thrilled by the immediate prospects of either going into graduate school right away or entering the workforce, read on. As I mentioned earlier, there are an abundance of good books targeted for recent college graduates. These books often cite opportunities and addresses of places you can visit and/or work after graduation. Your local library has many of these good books on its shelves, targeted specifically toward recent college graduates. For updated versions of these types of books, you may want to visit your local bookstore. Books on topics about the exciting opportunities recent college graduates have available to them are coming to bookstores nearly every day. Especially if you want to volunteer to work in another country, the opportunities are definitely there in abundance. A word of advice, however, and a word of caution are needed here: if you decide to take a lot of time off and you do not go into a graduate school program or full-time employment right away, you will have to explain to your future employer, or graduate school admissions, what you did during your time off. Unless you have spent your time either as a full-time volunteer or paid full-time employee, then your chances of either getting hired or being accepted into graduate school may be somewhat reduced.

Opportunities for recent college graduates to work abroad are endless. For example, if you would like to try your hand at teaching, you can apply to teach English in another country. Today, you even have a choice of where you would like to begin your teaching career. Would you prefer the tranquility of the rural Kenyan plains, or would the fast-paced, sprawling urban environment of Tokyo be more to your liking? Do you aim to make the world a better place for all people to live in? If you would like to help people in poorer nations, the opportunities are there. If you would like to work for international political organizations, including those of you aspiring to become diplomats, these work possibilities also exist. If you would like to help disabled or emotionally disturbed children, the opportunities and programs are there and are endless. All of these, and many more possibilities in the realm of volunteering exist.

## STEP 4: MAKE THE DECISION

The final, looming question that recent college graduates often face is the question of where to settle down and live after graduation. This is especially true for the traditional-age college student. Due to recent economic crunches, many college graduates have settled back in at their parents' house after graduation. This can happen if you do not mind or if you are comfortable with these living arrangements, or out of pure economic necessity. Probably few college graduates would feel that this living arrangement is a matter of choice. But, in reality, it really is. Many volunteer or paid work opportunities will pay for your travel and living expenses. If some do not, and receiving financial compensation is necessary for your well-being, then find another place to work for or volunteer. Be sure to check out your college's career center. They may know of programs that will help you get off to a solid financial start. Most career centers specialize in helping recent college graduates get off to a good start in the world of work.

Become actively involved in creating your own successful future after college. The person it takes to accomplish your goals is you. The resources are also in you, with a little help from your parents, teachers, advisors, and friends. The dedication, commitment, motivation, perseverance, and planning it takes to succeed in college come from within you. These characteristics will take you a long way after the last course has been completed, the last final handed in, and the last tassel turned over. Question: "What am I going to do with the rest of my life?" This time, I am certain you have some idea of where to begin searching for the answers.

# Appendix A: Sample List of Pros and Cons of Colleges (Idealistic vs. Realistic)

**I**nstructions: Be as honest as possible in your assessment. Go with your first gut instinct. Ask yourself these questions: "How important is each item in my decision to attend this college?" and "How closely does each item match those of my personality, interests, and goals?" You will probably want to visit each campus first and gather as much information about your prospective colleges before completing the following questionnaire. Because each college is different, use a separate response for each college you might attend. Add up your total score and divide by 10 to give you the average. An overall average score of less than 7 means you should reconsider attending that college. An overall average score of less than 5 means that you should discard that college choice immediately.

Use the following scale:

1 = extremely unimportant
2 = pretty unimportant
3 = unimportant
4 = somewhat unimportant
5 = neither important nor unimportant
6 = somewhat important
7 = important
8 = pretty important
9 = very important
10 = extremely important

- Quality of academic program/major you are interested in (if any)
- Political atmosphere (conservative/middle-of-the road/liberal)
- Social atmosphere (studious "geeky" school, "commuter school," "party school")
- Size of the college (small, medium, large)
- Location of the college (rural, small town, suburban, urban/city center)
- Availability/accessibility of instructors and academic advisors
- Campus resources (how closely do they have what you want?)
- Campus organizations (how closely do they match what you are interested in?)
- Financial aid assistance/availability at the college (if applicable to you or your parents)
- Overall feeling/gut instinct about the college

# Appendix B: Sample Questions to Ask Students during Your Visit/Tour

- What do you like most about University A?
- What do you hate most about University A?
- If you could change one thing about this university, what would it be?
- What was the most difficult part of campus life to adjust to when you first started going here?
- What was the easiest part of campus life to adjust to when you first started going here?
- If you had to describe this university using only one word, what would that word be?
- If you had to describe the students of this university using only one word, what would that word be?
- What is the best class you have taken at University A? What did you like the most about it?
- What is the worst class you have taken at University A? What did you hate the most about it?
- If you had to describe the typical professor here using only one word, what would that word be?
- If you could do it all over again, would you still choose to go here, to University A? Why would you choose to go here/not go here?

# Appendix C: Sample Schedule for Freshmen and Sophomores

*Year 1: Fall Semester*

| *Course Title* | *Semester hours* |
|---|---|
| Freshman Composition 1 | 3 |
| College Algebra | 3 or 4 |
| Foreign Language 1 | 3 |
| Introduction to Sociology | 3 |
| Introduction to Art Appreciation | 3 |
| Physical Education | 1 |
| Total Semester Hours | 16 or 17 |

*Year 1: Spring Semester*

| *Course Title* | *Semester hours* |
|---|---|
| Freshman Composition 2 | 3 |
| Advanced Mathematics course | 3 or 4 |
| Foreign Language 2 | 3 |
| Introduction to Biological Sciences | 4 |
| U.S. History, 1865–present | 3 |
| Physical Education | 1 |
| Total Semester Hours | 17 or 18 |

*Year 1: Summer Semester*

| Course Title | Semester hours |
| --- | --- |
| Foreign Language 3 | 3 |
| Foreign Language 4 | 3 |
| Total Semester Hours | 6 |

*Year 2: Fall Semester*

| Course Title | Semester hours |
| --- | --- |
| Advanced Mathematics | 3 or 4 |
| Foreign Language 5 | 3 |
| Introduction to Chemistry | 4 |
| Western Civilization 1 | 3 |
| Introduction to Psychology | 3 |
| Total Semester Hours | 16 or 17 |

*Year 2: Spring Semester*

| Course Title | Semester hours |
| --- | --- |
| Foreign Language 6 | 3 |
| Ethnic/Cultural Studies | 3 |
| Introduction to Astronomy | 4 |
| Western Civilization 2 | 3 |
| Introduction to Drawing/Painting | 3 |
| Total Semester Hours | 16 |

*Year 2: Summer Semester*

| Course Title | Semester hours |
| --- | --- |
| Study Abroad | 6 |
| Total Semester Hours | 6 |

# Appendix D: Pros and Cons of Transferring: Sample List

*Pros of Transferring*

1. I have decided to change my major. University A has a much better department in my major.
2. I have realigned my political attitudes dramatically, and I have found no support for my new political philosophy at my present school.
3. My present campus is in the city, and I have decided I do not like the city, or at least, this particular city, very much.
4. I am deeply dissatisfied with the department of my major.
5. My present campus is much too large. I would prefer a much smaller campus.
6. I am dissatisfied with the quality of education I am getting at my present school.

*Cons of Transferring*

1. I will miss the friends I have made here.
2. My present school has the cheapest tuition anywhere for a state university. Other schools will be much more expensive.
3. Maybe I can learn to like my college.

(*continued*)

*Pros of Transferring*                    *Cons of Transferring*

7. I simply do not have a good
   feeling for my present college.
   When I wake up in the
   morning, I absolutely dread
   going out onto the campus.

# Appendix E: Sample Letter to the Office of Admissions Expressing Your Interest in Transferring

1234 Old Oak Tree Way
Jacksonville, FL 32204

Office of Admissions
University of Florida
Gainesville, FL 32611

*Prospective Transfer Student*

Dear Sir or Madam,

Currently, I am a sophomore majoring in art at Florida Community College at Jacksonville. I am very interested in transferring to the University of Florida during my junior year. I would like to receive information from your office about how the courses I have taken/will be taking at Jacksonville will transfer to UF.

Specifically, would you mind sending me information on your transfer policies, including your acceptance of transfer credit, admission criteria and eligibility for new transfer students, and transfer course equivalencies at the University of Florida?

Also, if you could recommend a person I might be able to talk with about my desire to transfer to the University of Florida next fall, I would really appreciate it. Thank you very much for your guidance.

Sincerely,
John A. Smith

# Appendix F: Sample Resumes

The following is a sample resume for a current college student:

*Robert A. Jones*

| | |
|---|---|
| *School Address (September–May)* | *Permanent Address* |
| Room 101, Einstein Hall | 1234 Great Falls Blvd. |
| University of Washington | Olympia, WA 98507 |
| Seattle, WA 98195 | (360) 357-0000 |
| (206) 543-0000 | |

| | |
|---|---|
| *Objective* | To obtain an internship position in an international marketing firm that will utilize my educational background and allow for the fullest development of my abilities. |
| *Education* | University of Washington, Seattle, WA<br>Marketing Major, Dean's List, first 5 semesters.<br>Present grade point average 3.75/4.00.<br>Will graduate May 20—. |
| *Honors* | Phi Beta Kappa Business Honor Society<br>Dean's List (all 5 semesters completed)<br>Phi Beta Epsilon Spanish Language Society |
| *Related Courses* | International Marketing<br>International Business Economics<br>International Business Affairs |

| | |
|---|---|
| *Student* | Studied abroad in Madrid, Spain (Summer 20—) |
| *Activities* | Vice President of the International Business Association |
| | Secretary, Phi Beta Kappa Business Honor Society |
| | Spanish tutor on campus |
| *Experience* | *ABC Publishing Company*          Summer 20— |
| | Worked with computers processing returned books. |
| | *Quick Jobs Temporary Services*    Summer 20— |
| | Performed various data entry duties. |
| *References* | Available upon request. |

The following is a sample resume for a recent college graduate:

*Mary M. Smith*
1234 Buena Vista Drive
San Diego, CA 92093
(858) 534-0000

| | |
|---|---|
| *Objective* | To obtain a position as a Systems Analyst. |
| *Education* | University of California, San Diego |
| | B.S. Degree in Computer and Information Sciences, May 20— |
| | Major in Computer Science |
| | Cumulative GPA 3.45 |
| | *Relevant Courses:* |

| | |
|---|---|
| Information Processing Systems | Cobol |
| Accounting Information | Business Writing Systems |
| Managerial Accounting | Speech  Communications |
| Financial Accounting | Risk and Insurance |

| | |
|---|---|
| *Experience* | University of California,    August 20— to present |
| | San Diego |
| | *Laboratory Assistant—Center for Academic Computing* |
| | Duties include maintaining computer hardware and |
| | assisting users on IBM PS/2, IBM AS/400, and IBM |
| | VWCMS with various software packages. |

# Appendix G: College Program Sample: How to Graduate in a Minimum Amount of Time

**B**elow is my own goal list. Please keep in mind, however, that my choice of major, as well as the school I was attending, undoubtedly affected my minimal length of commitment. Your own goal list will probably differ, but writing a unique one for yourself will still help you to graduate within a reasonable amount of time.

## COLLEGE PROGRAM

Goal: To obtain a bachelor's degree within four years.
Date expected to achieve goal: December 1993
Major: Psychology

### 1st year 1990–1991 at California State University, Sacramento

*Fall 1990*

Major requirement—lower-division psychology
General education requirements—humanities, social science, American history
Physical education activity
Total hours = 13 semester

*Appendix G*

*Spring 1991*

Major requirement — lower-division psychology
General education requirements — English, social science (2), natural science
Total hours = 15 semester
Cumulative Total Hours = 28 semester


*Summer 1991 at De Anza Community College*

General education elective — humanities
Total hours = 4 quarter
Cumulative Total Hours = 46 quarter


**2nd year 1991–1992 at De Anza Community College**

*Fall 1991*

Major requirement — lower-division psychology
General education requirements — humanities (2)
Total hours = 12 quarter
Cumulative Total Hours = 58 quarter


*Winter 1992*

Major requirement — lower-division psychology
General education requirements — English, social science
Total hours = 13 quarter
Cumulative Total Hours = 71 quarter


*Spring 1992*

Major requirement — lower-division psychology
General education requirements — natural science, social science, cultural studies
Total hours = 18 quarter
Cumulative Total Hours = 89 quarter

*Summer 1992 De Anza Community College*

General education elective—English
Total hours = 5 quarter
Cumulative Total Hours = 94 quarter

## 3rd year 1992–1993 at University of California, Santa Cruz

*Fall 1992*

Major requirement—lower-division psychology
Major requirement—upper-division psychology
General education requirement—writing-intensive humanities
Total hours = 15 quarter
Cumulative Total Hours = 109 quarter

*Winter 1993*

Major requirements—upper-division psychology (2)
Major elective—upper-division psychology
General education requirement—cultural studies
Total hours = 20 quarter
Cumulative Total Hours = 129 quarter

*Spring 1993*

Major requirements—upper-division psychology (3)
General education elective—natural science
Total hours = 20 quarter
Cumulative Total Hours = 149 quarter

*Summer 1993 at De Anza Community College*

Major elective—lower-division psychology
General education electives—art (2)
Total hours = 10 quarter
Cumulative Total Hours = 159 quarter

## 4th year 1993–1994 at University of California, Santa Cruz

*Fall 1993*

Major electives—upper-division psychology (4)
Total hours = 20 quarter
Cumulative Total Hours = 179 quarter
Hours Needed to Graduate = 178 quarter

It can be done, as I have just shown you in the above diagram of the actual course requirements I fulfilled during my three-and-a-half years in college. However, it does take a good deal of planning and hard work.

# Glossary

**academic advisor:** College professionals whose job is to help students succeed in college. Academic advisors will typically help students plan their course schedule and help students search for a major. Some of these professionals also help students explore career goals and personal issues.

**career center:** An office in a college or university that usually assists students with career counseling, internship exploration, and sometimes job placement.

**commencement:** College or university graduation.

**community college:** A two-year college that usually offers freshman- and sophomore-level courses, including vocational courses, to the general public. *See also* junior college; two-year college.

**core requirements:** The prescribed course of study for freshmen and sophomores, typically consisting of the liberal arts curriculum of a college or university. *See also* general education requirements.

**credit hours:** How much a certain course is worth in terms of credit toward degree completion. Typically, an hour of credit is earned for every hour a student spends per week in class for a single course.

**dormitory:** Place of residence for college students, typically during the school year. *See also* residence hall.

**employment agency:** An office, typically located outside a college or university, whose staff assists with job placement and referrals for individuals seeking work.

**final examinations:** Exams usually given in every course at the end of each academic quarter or semester.

**general education requirements:** The prescribed course of study for freshmen and sophomores, typically consisting of the liberal arts curriculum of a college or university. *See also* core requirements.

**graduate students:** Students taking advanced, postbaccalaureate course work in a university.

**independent study:** Usually offers the chance for students to work one-on-one with a professor, outside of class, in order to conduct an in-depth study on a particular topic, often times to earn class credit and/or experience.

**internships:** Any work experience and/or training students can receive either within or outside of a college program. Internships typically provide students exposure to a particular field they are interested in exploring.

**junior college:** A college that usually offers freshman- and sophomore-level courses, including vocational courses, to the general public. *See also* community college; two-year college.

**liberal arts:** A prescribed course of study typically in the humanities, social sciences, and natural sciences.

**lower-division course:** Generally speaking, any class intended for freshman- and sophomore-level students. Usually can be taken by any college student, regardless of class level, provided course prerequisites have first been completed.

**major:** A prescribed intensive course of study of a single subject. Usually required for undergraduate students.

**minor:** A prescribed course of study of a single subject. Usually, a minor carries fewer credit hours than a major. Usually not required for undergraduate students.

**nontraditional student:** Undergraduate college student over age twenty-four, married of any age, or both.

**prerequisites:** Courses that students must complete prior to taking other, more advanced-level courses.

**quarter:** A type of academic calendar system a college or university operates on. Usually, there are three quarters per academic year. Each quarter is usually ten weeks long, plus a week of final examinations.

**research assistant:** Students who assist professors or graduate students with their research duties. Usually part of the college's course curriculum.

**residence hall:** Place of residence for college students, typically during the school year. *See also* dormitory.

**resume:** A document that shows the work history, education, and skills of a person. Usually submitted when applying for a job.

**semester:** A type of academic calendar system a college or university operates on. Usually, there are two semesters per academic year. Each semester is usually fifteen weeks long, plus a week of final examinations.

**teaching assistant:** Students who assist professors or graduate students with their teaching duties. Usually part of the college's course curriculum.

**traditional student:** Undergraduate college student under age twenty-four and single.

**transfer articulation agreement:** A written contract between a two-year junior or community college and a four-year college or university. The transfer articulation agreement basically specifies that a student will be admitted to the four-year college or university upon completion of specified course requirements and maintenance of a specified grade point average.

**transfer center:** An office within a two-year junior or community college that usually provides assistance to students wishing to transfer to a four-year college or university.

**transfer credit:** Courses that will generally transfer to another college or university.

**transfer student:** Any college student who moves to another college or university.

**two-year college:** A college that usually offers freshman- and sophomore-level courses, including vocational courses, to the general public. *See also* community college; junior college.

**upper-division course:** Generally speaking, any class intended for junior- and senior-level students. Usually can be taken by any college student, regardless of class level, provided course prerequisites have first been completed.

**vocational programs:** Generally speaking, any major outside of the liberal arts curriculum.

**volunteers:** Individuals who devote time and energy, often without pay, to certain organizations or to other individuals.

# Suggested Readings

Bury, H., et al. 2003. *College and Career Success Simplified*. Upper Saddle River, N.J.: Longman.

Carter, C. 1999. *Majoring in the Rest of Your Life: Career Secrets for College Students*. New York: Farrar, Straus & Giroux.

Combs, P., and J. Canfield. 2003. *Major in Success: Make College Easier, Fire Up Your Dreams, and Get a Very Cool Job*. 4th ed. Berkeley, Calif.: Ten Speed Press.

Gibbs, B. 2002. *Giving Away the Keys: A Professor Unlocks the Secrets to College Success*. Stone Mountain, Ga.: You Will Learn Publishers.

Groccia, J. 1992. *The College Success Book: A Whole-Student Approach to Academic Excellence*. Lakewood, Colo.: Glenbridge.

Newman, R. 1995. *The Complete Guide to College Success: What Every Student Needs to Know*. New York: New York University Press.

Williamson, J., D. McCandrew, and C. Muse. 2003. *Roadways to Success for Community College Students*. 3rd ed. Upper Saddle River, N.J.: Prentice Hall.

# About the Author

**Mark Mach** has held positions as an academic advisor and instructor at numerous institutions of higher education. In 1998, he completed a study of college student identity and adjustment to college among freshmen college students. Mach has served as an adjunct faculty member in psychology at California State University, San Bernardino; Skyline College in San Bruno, California; and Northwest Arkansas Community College in Bentonville, Arkansas. At the University of Arkansas, Mark advised undergraduate students with undeclared majors, students in preprofessional allied health fields, students in academic difficulty, and prospective college students. In 2002, he relocated to Thailand, where he taught university classes in managerial psychology, communications, and English. Mach currently serves as an academic advisor at the University of Kansas. In his free time, he enjoys traveling, reading, writing, and exploring the outdoors.